Whispers of
Encouragement
for Moms

Whispers of Encouragement *for* Moms

BARBOUR
PUBLISHING

Published by Barbour Publishing, Inc., P.O. Box 719, Uhrichsville, Ohio 44683, www.barbourbooks.com

Our mission is to publish and distribute inspirational products offering exceptional value and biblical encouragement to the masses.

Member of the
Evangelical Christian
Publishers Association

Printed in the United States of America.

Introduction

As a mom, you have the uncanny ability to do it all: to perform the tasks of counselor, nurse, chauffer, spiritual advisor, personal chef, friend, judge, negotiator, and housekeeper simultaneously. Whew—talk about a full-time job! Though the joys and triumphs of nurturing your family counter-balance all the stress and sleepless nights you've endured, self-doubt can be the hardest struggle of all for any mom to overcome. If you're in need of a word of encouragement today, you've come to the right place. Each page of this collection is packed with uplifting, real-life messages of hope, joy, and strength—all serving as a reminder that no matter what, God is there for you. You are His child, and He longs to care for and nurture you as one of His own. So sit back, relax, and take a little break! Surrender all your worries to Him and allow your Almighty Father to spoil you with His unending grace, wisdom, and love.

The Editors

Contents

Joy

To be a child is to know the joy of living.
To have a child is to know the beauty of life.

UNKNOWN

Happy Tears

My child, never forget the things I have taught you. . . .
A wise child brings joy to a father.

PROVERBS 3:1, 10:1 NLT

....

"It's just a book report—there's no reason to cry," the confused boy said to his mother.

Embarrassed by her sudden outburst, the mom quickly answered, "It's just that you're growing up so fast. It seems like only yesterday you were learning to walk, and now I see you're writing in cursive and. . . ." The tears started again.

"Mom, I didn't mean to make you sad," the boy said.

Mom replied, "I'm just so proud of you. These are tears of joy, not sadness. I'm so thankful to be your mom."

Sometimes we cry because we're sad. Other times we'll weep tears of joy and gratitude for the overwhelming privilege of being a mom. And not just any mom—their mom. We get so much satisfaction from watching our children learn from us and grow up under our care. Most rewarding of all, though, will be the day when we can enjoy the immense privilege of seeing them pass on their faith in the Savior to their kids.

Father God, there are no words to express my
thankfulness to You for the privilege of being my
children's mother. Thank You!

Making Memories

They shall abundantly utter the memory of thy great goodness,
and shall sing of thy righteousness.

PSALM 145:7 KJV

Scrapbooking has become a popular pastime for many American families. Something as simple as a trip to the ice cream shop can be transformed into a beautiful keepsake memory page. Everyday events become cherished lifelong memories to be enjoyed over and over again.

As the scrapbook pages turn, we move from potty training to the first day of school—then first dates. We reminisce over day trips to the park or living room campouts. We remember visits to the pet store and trips to the library. Those commonplace events that shape our children's memories become the cherished "good old days" to be shared with future generations.

The scrapbook, though, is only a vehicle. The essential thing is forming those memories! Let's purposefully create "snapshots" of our family times, bringing smiles to our kids' faces as they recall sweet memories of bike rides, homemade pancakes, or pillow fights in the living room.

May our little ones "abundantly utter the memory" of their childhood's goodness—and call to mind "the good old days" with their own children.

Father God, show me how to create memories for my children.
I long for them to treasure their childhood years.

Belly Laughs

All the days of the desponding and afflicted are made evil
[by anxious thoughts and forebodings], but he who has a glad
heart has a continual feast [regardless of circumstances].

PROVERBS 15:15 AMP

Do you know how to relax? Have you built a time for laughter into your schedule?

Maybe that sounds silly and unimportant with the demands of motherhood caving in on you. But it's not! In fact, relaxation and fun are vital to your health—and, by extension, the health of your family. We may face challenges, but as Proverbs reminds us, we can have a continual feast regardless of our circumstances. Don't wait for laughter to find you— seek it out!

Find a clean comedy show to loosen up. Maybe get into a tickling match with the kids. Perhaps it's as simple as scheduling a popcorn and movie night with the kids to melt away the day's pressure.

A good laugh is health to our bones and gives our kids permission to lighten up, too. Our families need to see us loosen up and enjoy ourselves now and then.

Heavenly Father, You are a God of laughter and enjoyment.
Why does it seem frivolous to giggle with my children?
Enable me to have a continual feast, regardless of my circumstances.

Joy Is Jesus

And even though you do not see [Jesus] now, you believe in him and are filled with an inexpressible and glorious joy, for you are receiving the goal of your faith, the salvation of your souls.

1 PETER 1:8–9 NIV

As children we find joy in the smallest things: a rose in bloom, a ladybug at rest, the ripples a pebble makes when dropped in water. Then somewhere between pigtails and pantyhose, our joy wanes and eventually evaporates in the desert of difficulties. But when we find Jesus, "all things become new" as the Bible promises, and once again we view the world through a child's eyes.

We learn that God's joy begins with the seed of God's Word planted in our hearts. Suddenly our hearts spill over with joy, knowing that God loves and forgives us and that He is in complete control of our lives. We have joy because we know this world is not our permanent home and a mansion awaits us in glory.

Joy comes as a result of whom we trust, not what we have. Joy is Jesus.

*Dear Jesus, thank You for giving me the joy of my salvation.
Knowing You surpasses anything and everything
else the world offers. Amen.*

Serendipity

A happy heart makes the face cheerful.

PROVERBS 15:13 NIV

Can you remember the last time you laughed in wild abandon? Better yet, when was the last time you did something fun, outrageous, or out of the ordinary?

Women often become trapped in the cycle of routine, and soon we lose our spontaneity. Children, on the other hand, are innately spontaneous. Giggling, they splash barefoot in rain puddles. Wide-eyed, they watch a kite soar toward the treetops. They make silly faces without inhibition; they see animal shapes in rock formations. In essence, they possess the secret of serendipity.

A happy heart turns life's situations into opportunities for fun. For instance, if a storm snuffs out the electricity, light a candle and play games, tell stories, or just enjoy the quiet. When we seek innocent pleasures, we glean the benefits of a happy heart.

Jesus said, "I am come that they might have life, and that they might have it more abundantly" (John 10:10 KJV). God wants us to enjoy life, and when we do, it lightens our load and changes our countenance.

So try a bit of whimsy just for fun. And rediscover the secret of serendipity.

Dear Lord, because of You, I have a happy heart.
Lead me to do something fun and spontaneous today! Amen.

She has achieved success who has lived well,
laughed often, and loved much.

BESSIE ANDERSON STANLEY

Joyful Songs

Sing joyfully to the LORD, you righteous;
it is fitting for the upright to praise him.

PSALM 33:1 NIV

Singing often reflects our mood. When we're lighthearted and happy, we tend to sing more often than when we're feeling burdened and downtrodden. But the Word of God tells us to sing joyfully to the Lord, without prerequisites. The Bible doesn't say, "Sing if all is well and you're overjoyed." It just tells us to sing joyfully.

It's fitting for us as Christians to praise Him. Not only when our circumstances are conducive to a joyful spirit, but any time—simply because of who He is.

If our actions depend on our situations, we may never try a tune. But if we sing amid our situation, whether good or bad, joyous or painful, we will soon find our moods—and our spirits—rising from the ashes to reflect our joyful songs.

When we, like the psalmist, sing joyfully to the Lord, our spirits will follow—and we'll become deeply joyful moms, unshaken and steady.

Lord, I know I need to sing to You out of a joyful spirit.
For all You have done for me,—and simply because of who
You are—I will choose today—whatever my circumstances—
to sing songs of praise, joy, and thanksgiving.

A Laugh a Day

On your feet now—applaud GOD!
Bring a gift of laughter, sing yourselves into his presence.

PSALM 100:1–2 MSG

There's an old saying that "laughter is the best medicine." But it's actually more than that. The Bible tells us that laughter is a *gift*. We should rejoice in the Lord and bring our gift of laughter to Him.

Sometimes, as a mom, you just have to laugh. Maybe you and your young son have just enjoyed a funny movie together. Or perhaps your teenage daughter thought it would be cool to dye her hair purple. In these cases, laughter can be both a song of praise and a catharsis.

It's important to find joy in the events of everyday life, and you should schedule time to pursue a good laugh after a tough week. Call some friends for a girls' night movie party or curl up with a funny book. Maybe you could listen to a Christian comedian for some good, clean humor and worship through laughter.

Whatever the source, make time to laugh—and send those giggles up to God.

Dear God, thank You for giving us the gift of laughter.
Help me to find joy in my daily life—
and to make time to laugh with family and friends.

Dance in Your PJs!

David, ceremonially dressed in priest's linen,
danced with great abandon before GOD.

2 SAMUEL 6:14 MSG

Is it really a matter of national importance if there are dirty clothes on the bedroom floor? Or if we allow the kids to eat cornflakes for dinner? Is it necessary to talk in our stern "mother voice" all the time?

King David had the audacity to be so happy, so full of joy that he danced in public. . .in his underclothes! Certainly he had his share of troubles and a plate full of responsibility—yet he found a way to enjoy himself as he worshipped God.

We'll probably encounter plenty of well-meaning people who remind us, "Raising children is not fun and games—this is serious business." And there's truth in that.

But parenting can be fun and games *sometimes.* Try this—plan a family pajama party or a living room campout, complete with a bedsheet tent.

Let's lighten up and enjoy this ride. It'll be over before we know it.

Father God, please help my children and me to relax—to enjoy
the life You've given us. Grant me creative ideas to simply
have fun and actually take pleasure in my family.

Million-Dollar Smile

A happy heart makes the face cheerful,
but heartache crushes the spirit.

PROVERBS 15:13 NIV

Ever seen a million-dollar smile? You know the one. It shines like the sun—and it's contagious. It makes everyone else light up, too.

Maybe the face encircling that smile is yours. Or maybe it's not. A million-dollar smile can't spread itself across a face weighed down by a broken heart or a wounded spirit. It can't be faked. You have to have happiness bubbling up from your heart in order to exhibit such a cheerful, honest smile. Where do you find that kind of happiness?

Only God can offer us joy—the true, long-lasting, nobody-can-take-it-away kind of joy that comes from knowing and trusting Him. We may carry a heavy load— but Jesus Christ wants to fill our hearts with joy so our faces shine like the morning sun.

Happy hearts are vital for us as moms. May our faces reflect the love of Christ in million-dollar smiles that spread like wildfire to the faces of our children.

Jesus, I want my cheerful face to speak of Your goodness. Though I've been hurt and I carry heavy burdens, I ask You to release my heartache. Please cause my face to be an expression of Your joy.

Life's Roller-Coaster Ride

"Live in me. Make your home in me just as I do in you. In the same way that a branch can't bear grapes by itself but only by being joined to the vine, you can't bear fruit unless you are joined with me."

JOHN 15:4 MSG

It's exhilarating to ride the first car of a roller coaster! Anticipation increases as the train slowly climbs to the top of the first hill. Nearing the pinnacle, excitement and fear grow in the riders. Then a thrilling descent followed by another uphill climb. People stand in line for the experience.

Parenting is a lot like that roller-coaster ride. We must enjoy each climb, savor the anticipation, and eagerly await the next hill we'll face.

So, who fills that seat beside us? Do we invite Jesus along as we climb the hills and hurtle into the valleys of life? Or is that seat always filled with friends, family members, or coworkers?

Make Jesus your constant companion. The ride will be richer and more memorable.

Jesus, forgive me for those times I leave You behind.
Be my constant companion, and help me to
enjoy and savor every moment.

Maternal love!
Thou word that sums all bliss.

ROBERT POLLOK

Action-Figure Easter

*We will not hide these truths from our children; we will tell the
next generation about the glorious deeds of the LORD.*

PSALM 78:4 NLT

Michelle opened the big picture Bible to Jesus' entry into
Jerusalem and smiled down at her children busily assem-
bling their props. Seven-year-old Michael spread palmetto
fronds across the toothpick road he'd carefully laid across
the floor. Five-year-old Kyla mounted the Jesus doll on her
toy pony and started down the winding path amid cries of
"Hosanna!" from her dad, who had lined a battalion of green
army men along the roadside. Toddler Josh clutched the
round pillow that would become the stone rolled in front of
the shoe-box tomb after Jesus' crucifixion on a cross formed
from pencils and rubber bands.

    This Good Friday tradition had begun when Michael
was in diapers and had evolved into a much-anticipated
family production. Michelle treasured her children's delight
each Easter morning when they sprang from their beds to
find the grave empty and Jesus miraculously sitting atop the
shoe-box tomb, his little plastic arms raised triumphantly in
the air.

*Risen Savior, help us use every opportunity to instill in
our children the marvelous truths of our faith, so that Your love
may be a precious heirloom to future generations. Amen.*

The Little Things

He blesses her with [children], and she is happy.
Shout praises to the LORD!

PSALM 113:9 CEV

She had been up all night. Her six-month-old baby had been crying for several hours now. She felt she'd reached her limit when something beautiful happened: The baby stopped wailing, and after a few minutes of rocking, both mother and child drifted off to sleep together.

Sometimes it feels as if this thing called "parenting" is the hardest, most thankless job around. But God reminds us in Psalm 113 that children are truly a blessing. They are His gift to us. The salvation of all humanity arrived in the form of a child—God's Son, Jesus Christ—who would grow up to pay the price for all our sins.

In the midst of the struggle, the little things—a smile, a laugh, a present from our children—can remind us how worthwhile this job of motherhood really is and how happy our children make us. Rejoice in these moments each day. Remember the continual blessings of children, the gift of parenthood, and the joy of both.

Dear heavenly Father, thank You for the gift of children.
Help me to rejoice in each moment of their lives—
especially when parenthood seems like a difficult task.
I praise You, Lord!

You Look Just Like. . .

*For those whom He foreknew [of whom He was aware and
loved beforehand], He also destined from the beginning
[foreordaining them] to be molded into the image of
His Son [and share inwardly His likeness].*

ROMANS 8:29 AMP

Family resemblance. We all have some resemblance to our
parents, even if we never saw them due to death or adop-
tion. It could be physical, like the shape of our nose, or it
could be in our mannerisms, like the way we walk or laugh.

When others tell us how much our children look like us
or act like us, we generally respond by saying, "Thank you."
For some reason, such comments elicit pride in us.

It's much the same in our Christian experience. Once
we've been brought into the family of God, we begin to take
on its defining characteristics. Through the Holy Spirit, we
are molded into the image of Christ, sharing His mind-set
and traits. Patience, kindness, compassion, and the desire to
please God gradually become part of who we are.

Just as we enjoy the resemblance our own children bear
toward us, our heavenly Father wants His children to "look
like" Him.

*Lord, please have Your way with me.
Cause me to bear the family resemblance.*

Choosing Wisely

Our mouths were filled with laughter.

PSALM 126:2 NIV

Amanda stared glumly at the rock-hard turkey parked on the kitchen counter. She'd miscalculated defrosting time; it was now Thanksgiving morning, and the entrée of honor was still obstinately ossified.

The twenty-two-pound bird was too large for the microwave, so she tried the blow dryer. Warm air only deflected into her face. Dunking the bird in a warm bathtub merely cooled the water down, and whacking the turkey with a hammer only intensified her budding headache.

Lunch was at noon. Guests would soon be arriving. What to do?

We women often plan perfect family events, only to find out how imperfectly things can turn out. Our reactions to these surprise glitches can make or break the event for everyone present.

The Bible says that Sarah laughed at the most unexpected, traumatic time of her life—when God announced that she would have a baby at the age of ninety (Genesis 18:12). At this unforeseen turn of events, she could either laugh, cry, or run away screaming.

She chose to laugh.

Lord, give us an extra dollop of grace and peace to laugh about unexpected dilemmas that pop up. And to remember that our reaction is a choice. Amen.

Fill 'er Up—with Joy

We also pray that you will be strengthened with all his glorious power so you will have all the endurance and patience you need. May you be filled with joy.

COLOSSIANS 1:11 NLT

We've all had days when we feel exhausted on every level, when we've drained our emotional gas tanks bone dry. We need a filling of God's strength so we can keep going—and rediscover *joy.*

But when can we find time to refill our tank in a life of constant work and worry? If we don't refuel, we'll stall out—and be of no use to anyone.

That means we have to learn to make time for ourselves. Some things, like listening to a favorite CD as we drift off to sleep, take no extra time. Others, like a bubble bath, may require minor adjustments to our schedule. There are many ways to recharge our spiritual batteries.

Every week—perhaps every day—we must set aside time to refill our tanks. The joy of the Lord will be our reward.

Lord of joy, we confess that we are tempted to work until we fall apart. We pray that You will show us the things that will give us the strength to go on.

The strength of motherhood is greater than natural laws.

BARBARA KINGSOLVER

Strength

Power in Weakness

God is my strength and power: and he maketh my way perfect.

2 SAMUEL 22:33 KJV

Being a disciplinarian and authority figure can be such a daunting task. We desperately desire our children to "like" us, yet realize some choices we make will not exactly endear us to them.

There are times when, no matter how much strength, willpower, and wisdom we muster, our power is insufficient. Our ability falls short of the need at hand. But that's okay. None of us are supermoms—able to leap mounds of dishes and piles of homework in a single bound, effortlessly handling board meetings, homework hassles, the supermarket dash, and upset tummies without breaking a sweat.

Thankfully our heavenly Father's strength is sufficient and equal to whatever task we face. He understands the pressures we face. He knows that we do not always feel competent for our life's challenges. So He beckons us to come to Him for strength, for direction, for patience and wisdom.

Father God, I am often left feeling overwhelmed and drained by the sheer responsibility before me. I cry out to You for my needs. Strengthen me and fill me with Your wisdom.

Feeling the Squeeze

The eye can never say to the hand, "I don't need you."
The head can't say to the feet, "I don't need you."

1 CORINTHIANS 12:21 NLT

We've all heard the term "the sandwich generation," referring to midlifers coping with teenagers on one end and aging parents on the other. Somehow calling it a sandwich sounds too easy. The in-between filling seems to fit comfortably, like ham and swiss on rye. A more appropriate term would be the "squeeze generation." Picture peanut butter and jelly oozing out of squished white bread.

It is a challenging season of life, and we can't do it alone. And perhaps that is a great blessing to realize. God never meant for us to do it alone! He designed us to live in communities—family, friends, and church—that help meet one another's needs. "The body is a unit," Paul told the believers at Corinth, "though it is made up of many parts; and though all its parts are many, they form one body. So it is with Christ" (1 Corinthians 12:12 NIV).

There's nothing wrong with asking for help when you need it.

Lord, You promise never to leave us nor forsake us.
Thank You for providing helpers to come alongside of me. Amen.

St–stuttering

"For if you forgive men when they sin against you, your heavenly Father will also forgive you. But if you do not forgive men their sins, your Father will not forgive your sins."

MATTHEW 6:14–15 NIV

Mary's young son stuttered when he talked. The doctor said he'd grow out of it, but Mary enrolled him in speech therapy anyway.

"I think I know why he stutters," volunteered Mary's opinionated mother-in-law. "You talk too fast."

Mary bit her tongue and tried to calmly explain that the part of the brain that controls speech was complicated and that she was doing everything she could to help her son. But her mother-in-law's remark felt like an arrow that hit a bull's-eye on a target: her insecurity at being a good mother.

Mary had a hard time forgiving her mother-in-law. Why was forgiveness so hard? Especially when the person who needed to be forgiven didn't seem to care?

In the Sermon on the Mount, Jesus encouraged His listeners to forgive offenders, but He didn't mention whether the offenders sought forgiveness. Jesus was only concerned about believers' obligations. We forgive because we are forgiven!

Lord, how often I ask You for forgiveness—and how readily You give it. May I never take for granted the gift of Your forgiveness. Amen.

Rip That Bandage Off!

"He has torn us, but He will heal us."

HOSEA 6:1 NASB

The young mother knew the old bandage needed changing—but her son just wouldn't cooperate. The child didn't understand why it had to come off—and he vehemently protested her attempts to remove the covering.

Finally the mother saw an opportunity and quickly ripped the bandage off. One moment of pain for the boy, and it was all over. Then she washed the wound, reapplied ointment and a fresh bandage, and set the boy on a path to full recovery.

Of course, in the son's eyes, his mother had callously caused him needless pain. He couldn't comprehend that the pain his mother had inflicted was for his *good*. . . .

So, too, our heavenly Father often allows pain as He seeks to bring healing to our lives. As He moves to heal our wounds, He may even cause pain that defies our understanding. But, as He reminds us through the prophet Hosea, there are times when God must tear in order to heal.

Lord, I haven't always recognized Your healing hand in my life. At times, I've only seen the tearing and screamed for it to stop. . . yet it was ultimately for my good. Thank You for healing me, Father.

Support Staff

Pile your troubles on GOD's shoulders—
he'll carry your load, he'll help you out.

PSALM 55:22 MSG

Moms are the unsung heroes, the support staff, the ones everyone depends on. Our purses hold everything from bandages to granola bars to tissues. If you need it, we'll find it. But there are days when we tire of carrying the weight of the world. Sometimes we run ourselves ragged taking care of everyone—everyone, that is, except for ourselves.

There came a time when Elijah grew tired of caring for Israel. Worn out, he ran for the hills, contemplating early retirement. In fact, he hoped God would give him a break and end it all. "Just kill me," Elijah begged God. He was *that* exhausted.

Was God angry with Elijah for seeking an escape? Did God stand over Elijah, wagging a finger, telling him to pull it together?

Just the opposite! Tenderly, oh so tenderly, God sent angels to care for Elijah. They provided food and rest and encouragement.

Sometimes we're so busy and tired we have nothing left to give. During those times, remember Elijah. Rest, eat, nourish yourself. Just let God be in charge for a while.

Dear Lord, teach me to ask for help. Prod me to take better care of myself. Thank You for Your gentle response to my low periods. Remind me that things will get better again! They always do.

A mother is and must be—whether she knows it or not—the greatest, strongest, and most lasting teacher her children have.

HANNAH WHITALL SMITH

Finding Strength in Silence

*For thus says the Lord God, the Holy One of Israel:
"In returning and rest you shall be saved; in quietness
and confidence shall be your strength."*

ISAIAH 30:15 NKJV

Long days, frantic schedules, and the ever-increasing demands of work and home can crowd God completely out of
our minds—and weary us to the bone.

We plan and anticipate troubles with money, work,
and our children. . .yet we are never quite prepared enough.
Something always comes up, making our lives a touch more
difficult and exhausting. Too many times there is just not
enough mom to go around.

That's when we need to remember that our true
strength never comes from our own efforts. Our sure rest
isn't something that we create. According to Bible schol-
ars, "quietness and confidence" in this verse can also mean
"utter trust." Only when we rely on God and spend time
with Him does comfort find a way into our everyday world.
Trusting in God's strength is the only way to true rest and
success.

*Father God, You care for us so much! When we let the whirl-
winds of life crowd You out, help us remember that only by trusting in Your love and grace do we find true strength and rest.*

Lacking Nothing

Consider it pure joy, my brothers, whenever you face trials of many kinds, because you know that the testing of your faith develops perseverance. Perseverance must finish its work so that you may be mature and complete, not lacking anything.

JAMES 1:2–4 NIV

Trials are never fun. But they're still necessary.

When people speak of trials, they might be referring to anything—from sleep deprivation to the loss of a loved one, to anything in between. How can we "consider it pure joy" when we face such trials? It's not the trial itself that we celebrate but the personal growth and expansion of our faith that can lead to joy.

Trials don't get easier from one to the next. But when we get through one—battered but not broken—we can take that growth and strength we gain and apply it to the next trial. We become better equipped to face the next obstacle with perseverance, comfort, and hope. And we can walk straight ahead, knowing that in the end we will be mature and complete, lacking absolutely nothing in Christ Jesus.

Abba Father, I know You go with me through these trials. Increase my joy through these trials and help me remember the purpose of them—that I may not lack any good thing.

Keeping a Promise

"I prayed for this child, and the Lord has granted me what I asked of him. So now I give him to the Lord. For his whole life he will be given over to the Lord."

1 Samuel 1:27–28 NIV

How did Hannah feel as she handed Samuel over to Eli, the priest, to raise? Did she worry over what kind of surrogate parent Eli would be for her boy? After all, Eli's own sons, also priests, were labeled "wicked men" (1 Samuel 2:12 NIV).

Years before, Hannah had begged God to bless her with a child. In return, she relinquished the child to the Lord's service. Amazingly, as she left the temple with empty arms, Hannah sang a song of praise and thanksgiving to God (1 Samuel 2:1–10). She was grateful to the God who answered her prayer and trusted Him with Samuel's life, even while he lived among Eli's wicked sons. And Samuel came out just fine—he became the spiritual leader of Israel for many years!

Our kids will encounter bad influences, too—even in good places. Can we trust God confidently, like Hannah did, resting assured that they belong to Him?

Lord, when situations are out of my control,
I thank You that You are always in control.

More than Enough

Let us not become weary in doing good, for at the proper time we will reap a harvest if we do not give up.

GALATIANS 6:9 NIV

How often do we become impatient and give up? We stand in line at the coffee shop and find ourselves behind an indecisive person. Frustrated, we give up—only to see that person—coffee cup in hand—walking past as we head to the car. If we'd only waited another minute, we, too, could be sipping a steaming caramel latte.

Or maybe we have a dream that we can't seem to make a reality—and rather than trying again, we give up. The Word of God encourages us to keep going, to fight off weariness and never give up. Jesus Christ has a harvest for each of us, and we can only imagine what it might be, because we know that God is the God of "immeasurably more than all we ask or imagine" (Ephesians 3:20 NIV).

When you're tired, keep going—and remember that, in His perfect timing, you will reap an unimaginable harvest.

Father, You know that I'm tired and weary in this uphill struggle. Fill me with Your strength so I can carry on. I long to reap the harvest You have for me.

The Promise of Joy

Weeping may endure for a night, but joy cometh in the morning.

PSALM 30:5 KJV

Have you experienced suffering? Perhaps you are hurting even now. Tough times are a reality for all of us.

The psalmist David was well acquainted with hardship. Although he was known as a man after God's own heart, at times David was pursued by his enemies and forced to run for his life. He also lived with the consequences of committing murder and adultery long after receiving God's forgiveness. But God is faithful and suffering is temporary. This is a promise we can claim, as David did, when facing difficulty or depression.

As believers we can find joy in the Lord even as certain trials persist in our lives. All suffering will end one day when we meet Jesus. The Bible assures us that in heaven there will be no tears.

Your loving heavenly Father has not forgotten you. You may feel that relief will never come, but take courage. It will.

God, where there is anguish in my life, may Your joy enter in. I ask for grace to face my trials, knowing that in time You will replace weeping with joy. Amen.

If you would have your children to walk honorably through the world, you must not attempt to clear the stones from their path but teach them to walk firmly over them—not insist upon leading them by the hand but let them learn to go alone.

ANNE BRONTË

Steady Hands

I have set the LORD always before me.
Because he is at my right hand, I will not be shaken.

PSALM 16:8 NIV

What shakes you? For moms, the list can be unending.

Whatever the circumstances, remember that the Lord is at your right hand! In the Bible the "right hand" symbolizes the kingship of God. He's the King of all kings, the ruler and ultimate authority over everything. And you know what? He holds your right hand and steadies your foundation.

Since God knows the beginning and the end, He's acutely aware of what we can handle. And He'll never allow even a smidgen more than we can take.

The Lord never said He'd take our hard times away. But at just the perfect time He'll supply exactly what we need to get through the earthquakes of life. He'll lead us safely to a place that's solid and firm.

With Christ at our right hand, we need never be shaken.

Jesus, please take my hand and steady my walk.
When my circumstances are shaky, be my firm foundation, Lord.

Carry On

It is God who arms me with strength and makes my way perfect.

Psalm 18:32 NIV

How often do we become overwhelmed with our difficult circumstances or feel as if our strength has been sapped to rock bottom?

We often find ourselves sleep deprived, our strength swirling rapidly down the drain like soapy bathwater. We become acutely aware that we can do nothing in our own strength—that raising kids takes enormous emotional, physical, and mental stamina.

It's at that point that we realize where our real source of power lies—in God, who arms us with strength and makes our way perfect. He is the One who fills our spirit with the desire to keep praying, even when we've seen no results. He is the One who helps us get up in the morning and face the new day, when we really want to pull the covers over our heads and sleep till next week.

It is God who arms us with strength—His amazing, mind-boggling strength.

God, I believe Your Word, so I am asking You for power for today.
I thank You for making my way perfect and for
arming me today with strength.

Hunks of Rust

Then Deborah said to Barak, "Go! This is the day the LORD has given Sisera into your hands. Has not the LORD gone ahead of you?"

JUDGES 4:14 NIV

For twenty years Sisera had cruelly oppressed the Israelites. He had a fleet of nine hundred iron-plated chariots that caused dread among the Israelites. Small wonder no one challenged him.

But then the Lord told the prophet Deborah it was time for Israel to confront Sisera. General Barak was tapped to lead the charge—but he refused! He insisted that Deborah come with him. So she did—and in a brilliant stroke, God sent rain! Lots and lots of rain. Oozing mud gripped Sisera's chariots like sticky glue.

Despite Barak's doubt about going into battle, Deborah knew that God was sovereign over all things, including the weather! Those iron chariots turned into big hunks of rust.

How do we look at dire circumstances? Do we see only the obstacles? Hopefully we have the faith to believe that God can turn any situation into a victory. After all, as Deborah reminded Barak, has not the Lord gone ahead of us?

Lord, the very things we fear the most are nothing to You! You are sovereign over everything. Thank You for going ahead of me and leading me to victory.

The Discipline Dilemma

*O LORD. . .your laws are righteous, and in faithfulness
you have afflicted me. . . . Before I was afflicted
I went astray, but now I obey your word.*

PSALM 119:75, 67 NIV

Let's face it: We want our children to rely on us, to like us,
to want to be with us more than anyone else.

But the I-want-my-kids-to-like-me syndrome can
cause some parents to recoil from even the thought of
much-needed discipline. Sometimes we wrongly assume
that discipline gets in the way of showing our children love.
But the reality is that a lack of discipline is unkind and
unloving.

"Before I was afflicted I went astray," scripture says, "but
now I obey your word." Affliction, apparently, is one thing
that created a change in this psalmist's behavior.

It's okay to "afflict" our children—with a loss of privi-
leges or a few extra chores—to teach them a lesson. Of
course our little darlings may not like us at that moment.
But, ultimately, we are showing more genuine love than any
amount of "friendship parenting" ever would.

*Heavenly Father, I lean on and rely on You to
help me parent my child. Grant me wisdom to know
when and what kind of discipline to use.*

Never Alone

There stood by the cross of Jesus his mother, and his mother's sister, Mary the wife of Cleophas, and Mary Magdalene.

JOHN 19:25 KJV

Mary breathed every agonizing breath with Jesus as soldiers tortured Him on the cross.

He is the King of the Jews! She tried to recall the angel Gabriel's announcement, old Simeon's prophecies, the wise men's worship. . .all affirmations of Jesus' divine nature. But all she saw was her dying Son.

However, God did not allow Mary to cry alone. Although other disciples hid, John, at Jesus' request, cared for Mary like his own mother. Despite possible danger, Mary's female friends refused to desert her or Jesus. Brave Nicodemus and Joseph of Arimathea asked Pilate for His body. Mary Magdalene, Joanna, and others tried to assist at His burial.

While few mothers share Mary's horrible experience, all of us hurt when our children struggle. Like her, we may not understand their suffering or senseless humiliation, thinking, *Where is God?*

He is there in the tears, hugs, and loving care of friends. And, like Mary, He knows how a Son's pain feels.

Father, when I watch my children grapple with life or death, You never leave me alone. Thank You.

A happy family is but an earlier heaven.

GEORGE BERNARD SHAW

Peace

Perfect Prayers

Pray, therefore, like this: Our Father. . . .
Out of the depths have I cried to You, O Lord.

MATTHEW 6:9 AMP; PSALM 130:1 AMP

How many messages have you heard on prayer? Have you ever come away thinking, *Did you hear how eloquently they prayed? How spiritual they sounded? No wonder God answers their prayers!*

Sometimes we take the straightforward and uncomplicated idea of prayer—the simple give-and-take of talking with God—and turn it into something hard.

Just pour out your heart to God. Share how your day went. Tell Him your dreams. Ask Him to search you and reveal areas of compromise. Thank Him for your lunch. Plead for your kids' well-being. Complain about your car. . . . Just talk with Him. Don't worry how impressive (or unimpressive!) you sound.

Talk with God while doing dishes, driving the car, folding laundry, eating lunch, or kneeling by your bed. Whenever, wherever, whatever—tell Him. He cares!

Don't allow this day to slip away without talking to your Father. No perfection required.

Father God, what a privilege it is to unburden my heart to You.
Teach me the beauty and simplicity of simply
sharing my day with You.

Blessings or Burdens?

The people brought children to Jesus, hoping he might touch them.
The disciples shooed them off. But Jesus was irate and let them
know it: "Don't push these children away."

MARK 10:13–14 MSG
....

"Did you get your homework done?" "Clean your room!"
"Stop teasing your sister!" "No, you cannot have potato chips
for dinner." "If I have to change one more diaper, I'm gonna
scream."

Sound familiar?

Not exactly the picture-perfect family scenario you were
hoping for—but this is reality.

Like all of us, Jesus had a busy schedule. Yet He took
time for children. Think about it—the Lord of glory
bounced kids on His lap! The disciples tried to shoo the
children away. After all, there were more important matters
to attend to, and they couldn't be bothered by giggling kids
with runny noses.

Are we sometimes so caught up in "being mom" that
we forget to stop and enjoy the moments we have with our
children? Would a potato chip dinner over a board game
knock us out of the running for "Mom of the Year"?

Let's make sure our children know they're not a burden
but a blessing.

Father God, what a blessing You have given me in my children.
Teach me how to enjoy my time with them.

Letting Go, Letting God

"This is the word of the GOD of Israel: 'The jar of flour will not run out and the bottle of oil will not become empty before GOD sends rain on the land and ends this drought.'"

1 KINGS 17:14 MSG

Too many times the only peaceful moments in the day are when the children are asleep. Tucked away at last, their faces relax and their cares melt away. Mom's worries, however, are not so easily set aside.

Being a mother means worrying about our children: their health, success in school, and friend selections.

In the Bible, the widow of Zarephath had an even sharper concern. She had only enough flour to make one more meal for herself and her son. Yet Elijah urged her to make that flour into a biscuit for *him*—with God's promise that, if she did, her food would never run out. She chose to trust, to turn her life and the life of her son over to the Lord.

Turning *our* children over to God isn't easy, but the Lord who helped a desperate widow three thousand years ago remains by our side today.

Father God, help us remember that You care for our children intimately and eternally. Remind us that You will not let us fall.

Rock of Ages

*You will guard him and keep him in perfect and constant peace
whose mind [both its inclination and its character] is stayed on
You, because he commits himself to You, leans on You, and hopes
confidently in You. So trust in the Lord (commit yourself to Him,
lean on Him, hope confidently in Him) forever; for the Lord God
is an everlasting Rock [the Rock of Ages].*

ISAIAH 26:3–4 AMP

You and I can have peace. Authentic peace. God-breathed
peace. Not because we live in some make-believe world,
repeating positive-thinking statements in an attempt to alter
reality. Not because we've been able to avoid adversity or
opposition. No, we can have peace simply and only because
we trust our heavenly Father.

God calls us to lean confidently on Him and His faithfulness, rather than fretting over our circumstances. This
doesn't imply that we'll live without difficulties. But when
we make the commitment to trust our heavenly Father, He
guards us and keeps us in His peace.

No matter what hardship we face, God is our solid
Rock. . .our Rock of Ages.

*Father God, grant me the ability to trust You, come what may.
Cause my eyes to focus on You, not the challenges I face.*

A mother's arms are made of tenderness, and children sleep soundly in them.

VICTOR HUGO

Just Say No

*"You're going to wear yourself out—and the people, too.
This job is too heavy a burden for you to handle all by yourself."*

EXODUS 18:18 NLT

Jennifer, a pediatrician and mother of two preschoolers, had to learn how to "just say no."

When she was finally able to conceive after years of frustration, she knew she had to make a choice. It was motherhood or doctorhood. Jennifer knew her limits. She chose motherhood.

Jennifer loves to lead women's Bible studies. And she's good at it. Now that she has two sons, however, she's had to say no. Jennifer knows her limits.

Unlike Jennifer and like Moses, many of us try to do it all. We want to fix what is not fixable. Important things need to be done, and if we do them, we're certain they will be done right. But we can't do it all. We, too, have to learn to say no sometimes—without guilt and without apology.

What God gives us grace and strength to do, let's do wholeheartedly. But let's learn to "just say no," too.

Lord, give me the wisdom I need to say yes and the discernment I need to say no. Amen.

Be with Jesus

*The officials were amazed to see how brave Peter and John were,
and they knew that these two apostles were only ordinary men
and not well educated. The officials were certain
that these men had been with Jesus.*

ACTS 4:13 CEV

The third grader needs help with his multiplication tables,
the spaghetti is boiling over, the phone is ringing, and the
baby just threw applesauce on the wall.

With all the concerns and distractions of motherhood,
it's easy to get so busy that we overlook our need to spend
time with Jesus.

Others can tell when we've made time for Jesus. He'll
give us bravery for our tasks but also love, joy, self-control,
and peace. The "officials" of Acts 4:13 were amazed not
by Peter and John's education, wealth, or status but simply
because it was obvious they had been with Jesus.

Each morning as we seek Jesus, let's not just give Him
a list of our needs for the day. Let's listen to what He wants
to tell us and praise Him for who He is. The results will be
amazing!

*Dear Jesus, help me not to be so busy that I push You aside.
I love You for who You are. Shine through me today
so others can be amazed by You.*

On the Back Burner

Based on the gift they have received, everyone should use it to serve others, as good managers of the varied grace of God.

1 PETER 4:10 HCSB

There is a season for everything in our lives. But shelving that haven of creativity that fills and reenergizes us isn't what God intended. He wants us to use our gifts and share them with others. We might even miss an opportunity by leaving some of our talents out of our motherhood—our art or music, cooking or gardening, writing or playing a sport.

Pursue creativity with your children. Cook with them. Pick up a crayon, and color with them. Grow a garden with them. Learn a new skill together. Let your kids see that you value your own creative spark. It doesn't have to be an enormous endeavor or result in a masterpiece. But pursuing our God-given creativity sets an example—of taking pleasure in God's gift.

God observed His own work of creation and declared it was "very good." Creativity is a wonderful gift that reflects God's image to our kids and our world.

Lord of all, You gave me a creative spark to use! Show me how to keep that flame alive and nourished, to benefit myself and my family.

Peanut Butter and Jelly

A meal of bread and water in contented peace
is better than a banquet spiced with quarrels.

PROVERBS 17:1 MSG

You've just cooked the perfect meal and are ready to sit down, relax, and eat. . . . But then the kids come to the table, bickering and pushing each other. You settle things down momentarily then hear an under-the-table kick followed by a scream.

At this point, do you still feel like eating that wonderful meal? Proverbs 17 says it would be better for a family to dine on bread and water in peace than on a huge feast when everyone is unhappy and fighting.

If you find yourself in the latter situation more often than not, maybe it's time for the bread and water. Instead of devoting time to an elaborate meal, just sit at the table together with a loaf of bread and jars of peanut butter and jelly. Talk, share, and prepare the evening meal together.

Your family will live through the night without a three-course dinner. And, just maybe, the extra time together around more simple fare will reap bountiful rewards of contented peace.

Heavenly Father, please bring peace to my home.
Calm the bickering and the strife. Unite us in You so that we can
enjoy one another.

Shake It Off

*Then [Paul simply] shook off the small creature
into the fire and suffered no evil effects.*

ACTS 28:5 AMP

How many times do we make a mistake and confess it to
the Lord then continue to punish ourselves with guilt and
condemnation? Psalm 103:12 tells us that God will remove
our transgressions as far as the east is from the west.

By immediately shaking a snake off his hand, Paul
avoided harm. The viper's intentions were to infect Paul with
poison and make him ill. Paul recognized the danger and
immediately went into action, shaking it off. Afterward he
didn't worry over it. Instead he went about helping the people
on the island of Malta.

Don't allow your mistakes to so worry or condemn you
that you can't be helpful to others around you. The poison of
stress and worry will harm us if we allow it to penetrate our
hearts and minds. Follow Paul's example: Shake it off.

*Dear Lord, thank You for cleansing me of my sins.
I will not worry or feel condemned any longer. Thank You, Lord,
for helping me to shake things off and suffer no evil effects.*

A mother is the one through whom God whispers love to His little children.

UNKNOWN

Finding Balance

But the Lord said to her, "My dear Martha, you are worried and upset over all these details! There is only one thing worth being concerned about. Mary has discovered it, and it will not be taken away from her."

LUKE 10:41–42 NLT

With people in the house needing to be fed, Martha jumped in to accomplish her tasks. Mary, on the other hand, chose to spend time in the presence of Jesus.

Because of Mary's choice, Martha had to do all the work by herself. She was even chastised for criticizing Mary. But if Martha hadn't done that work, who would have?

The two sisters from Bethany are a perfect example of the inner struggle that most women face daily. On one hand, we want to multitask and get things done. On the other hand, we crave rest, spiritual growth, and peace. The challenge is to blend the two into a healthy whole.

God has called us to good deeds but not to stress and worry. Ask Him to show you the line.

Dear Lord, I want to do my part, like Martha—but, like Mary, I also need to be strong enough to say no in order to have time with You. Please show me how to find that balance in my life.

Have You Looked Up?

*The heavens proclaim the glory of God. The skies display his
craftsmanship. Day after day they continue to speak;
night after night they make him known.*

PSALM 19:1–2 NLT

One afternoon Cathy was walking around the park near her
home. Her mind whirred with concerns about work and
worries about her kids.

Suddenly a man called out, "Hey lady! Have you looked
up?"

She stopped and turned to see who was shouting. The
voice belonged to an elderly man seated on a bench.

"Have you looked up?" he asked her again.

She lifted her head and saw a magnificent scarlet oak
tree, with leaves of crimson at the peak of their color. It was
so beautiful that it took her breath away. She thanked the
man and resumed her walk, relaxed and grateful after being
reminded to "look up!"

God has placed glimpses of creation's majesty—evidence
of His love—throughout our world. Sunsets, seashells, flowers, snowflakes, moonlit shadows. Such glories are right in
front of us, every single day! But we must develop eyes to see
these reminders in our daily life.

Have you looked up today?

*Lord, open my eyes! Teach me to see the wonders of Your
creation every day and to point them out to my children.*

Contentment?
Yeah, Right. . .

*Be anxious for nothing, but in everything by prayer
and supplication, with thanksgiving, let your
requests be made known to God.*

PHILIPPIANS 4:6 NKJV

The pan flew across the room, hitting the wall and dropping to the floor with a thud. Two squabbling kids at the dinner table stared at their young mother, who stood with tears streaming down her face. "Go to your rooms," she said quietly, as she bent to pick up the pan. They fled.

"Lord," she whispered, "I can't do this anymore."

Most moms can relate. Sooner or later almost all of us get pushed to the brink, and scripture lessons on "being content in all things" begin to sound hollow and trite.

Yet we may miss Paul's true message when he writes about contentment. Believers are not necessarily meant to be content *with* all circumstances but *in* all circumstances. And being content does not guarantee improvement; rather it's an understanding that God will always provide a way for us to work through our problems.

Commit problems to God in prayer and trust that He will provide deliverance. And thus peace.

*Father God, when things are hard, help me remember that peace
comes not from accepting where I am but from trusting You will
always provide for me.*

Starry Skies

Lift your eyes and look to the heavens: Who created all these?
He who brings out the starry host one by one, and calls them
each by name. Because of his great power and mighty strength,
not one of them is missing.

ISAIAH 40:26 NIV

Everyone should spend some time stargazing. When we slow
the frantic pace of our minds and look to the heavens, we begin to sense the unmatchable power, the sustaining strength,
and the intimate love of God. As we gaze with admiration
at the stars, we can drink in the very essence of our heavenly
Creator.

It was God who hung every star in place. It's God who
knows each star by name. Nothing in the farthest reaches of
the universe goes unnoticed by God, because He's a God of
order and intimacy.

If God cares that deeply about His starry creation, how
much greater is His love for us, His cherished daughters?

Father, You are the Creator of all. I thank You that I
can take in the awesome vastness of the universe and
rest in peace—knowing that You are not only the
Master Creator but that You hold me.

Basking in God's Presence

By day the LORD went ahead of them in a pillar of cloud. . .
and by night in a pillar of fire to give them light.

EXODUS 13:21 NIV

How soothing it must have been to those Israelites to feel the warmth of the pillar of fire in the cold desert night. How comforting to be sheltered from the blazing hot sun with a pillar of cloud by day. Imagine how it must have been to have such a visible symbol of God's company among His people. They were literally able to bask in the presence of God.

Even better than a visible pillar is the gift of the indwelling Holy Spirit—especially for moms! The Spirit empowers us to obey God's Word, teaches us to grow in maturity of character, comforts, counsels, and ministers to us.

The indwelling of the Holy Spirit is better than any external symbol of God. Unlike the Old Testament holy pillar—remarkable but temporary—the Holy Spirit will never depart from us.

Lord, in all of my family's struggles, may we sense Your nearness.
Please show us that You really are closer than our own breath
and that You see and hear everything that happens.

The hardest job you'll ever love is being a mother.

UNKNOWN

Hope

God of Hope

I pray that God, the source of hope, will fill you completely with joy and peace because you trust in him. Then you will overflow with confident hope through the power of the Holy Spirit.

ROMANS 15:13 NLT

In our busy, fast-paced lives, we may feel exhausted at times. Constantly putting out fires and completing tasks, working incessantly, we may feel discouraged and disheartened with life. There is more to life than this, isn't there?

Our God of hope says, *"Yes!"* God desires to fill us to the brim with joy and peace. But to receive these gifts, we need to have faith in the God who says, "Anything is possible if a person believes" (Mark 9:23 NLT). We need to place our confidence in God who, in His timing and through us, will do whatever it is we need. The key is recounting God's faithfulness out loud, quietly in your heart, and to others. When you begin to feel discouraged and exhausted, *stop*; go before the throne of grace, and recall God's faithfulness.

God of hope, I recount Your faithfulness to me.
Please fill me with Your joy and peace, because I
believe You are able to accomplish all things. Amen.

New Every Day

"See, I am doing a new thing!
Now it springs up; do you not perceive it?"

ISAIAH 43:19 NIV

One of the blessings of motherhood is watching our children grow. Changes come quickly in infancy—the first tooth, the first word, the first step. Later we see the first friendship, the first day at school, the first line in a class play. Eventually our precious babies will become teenagers, head off to high school, and then leave home. Then we'll get to enjoy the process all over again, as grandmothers.

God wants us to approach all of life with the same fresh wonder. If every baby affirms that God wants the world to go on and every rainbow is a reminder of God's promise, every dawn represents a new start.

In fact, God gives us countless opportunities to start over. The word *new* appears over 150 times in the Bible. Instead of worrying about the past, God wants us to long for what will be. He is the God of all things new.

Eternal God, every day is a new opportunity from You.
Teach me to rejoice in what You promise us.

He's Watching!

*The eyes of the LORD are on the righteous
and his ears are attentive to their cry.*

PSALM 34:15 NIV

Does it seem strange to think that God is watching everything we do? As if He's a traffic cop, hiding behind a billboard, waiting to catch us doing something wrong?

Replace that mental image with the memory of the first time you held your baby in your arms. Or when you watched your child play at a playground. Or act in a school play. Or sing in the church choir. Your eyes scanned the crowd, searching for that familiar little face. You couldn't keep your eyes off your baby. *That child belongs to me!* you thought.

God is watching each one of us with the same intense love with which we watch our children. His ability to be near us every moment is no threat—it's a promise. A guarantee! His Word tells us that He is near to everyone who calls out His name. We belong to Him! He can't keep His eyes off us.

Lord, why is it so hard to believe that You love me? Your Word reassures me, over and over, yet still I doubt. Remind me again, Lord. Convince me! Draw close! Open my eyes to Your presence.

God's Exchange Policy

To appoint unto them that mourn in Zion, to give unto them beauty for ashes, the oil of joy for mourning, the garment of praise for the spirit of heaviness. . .that [the LORD] might be glorified.

ISAIAH 61:3 KJV

When the sale was on, the cute shoes with too-high heels seemed perfect. The coat in that odd shade of green appeared an incredible bargain. At home, however, the coat and shoes didn't look so great. *What was I thinking?*

So you stand in a long line, hoping to exchange them over your lunch hour. But the receipt's in your other purse. Will you receive the full price back without it? Do they even accept a return on sale items? You glance at a calendar. Does the store place a time limit on returns?

God's exchange policy as recorded in Isaiah seems too good to be true. No standing in line. No hassles. For the ashes of our pasts, He offers a beautiful future. We've grown accustomed to dark, depressing clothes, but He points us to dressing rooms where new outfits await: garments of praise—light, lovely dresses that fit us perfectly.

Lord Jesus, what an exchange! I want to wear this garment of praise every day, just for You.

In Whom We Have Hope

May the God of hope fill you with all joy and peace as you trust in him, so that you may overflow with hope by the power of the Holy Spirit.

ROMANS 15:13 NIV

It's surprising what trials people get through if they have hope.

We know how difficult life can be when, for example, our kids come down with chicken pox. The babysitter won't take children with a contagious illness, and the boss won't allow more than two days off work. Face it—in a situation like that, you're stuck. Is it possible to have peace and joy in such circumstances? Yes! That is, if you have hope.

But not just any old hope. The power of hope arises from "the God of hope," as Romans 15:13 says. Hope in our jobs, our finances, our babysitters, or even our own family members often falls flat.

No matter what happens, He can fill us with overflowing joy and perfect peace.

God, in the midst of my circumstances, please teach me to put my hope in You. I look to You to fill me with joy and perfect peace.

The only rock I know that stays steady, the only institution I know that works is the family.

LEE IACOCCA

A New Day

God, treat us kindly. You're our only hope. First thing in the morning, be there for us! When things go bad, help us out!

ISAIAH 33:2 MSG

There are days that start off wrong and finish worse. We experience days full of failure, tinged by sin.

Luckily we have an opportunity to redo our bad days. It's called *tomorrow*. Lamentations 3:22–23 tells us that by God's mercy, He gives us a fresh canvas every twenty-four hours. No matter how stormy the day before, each day starts brand-new. And He is there for us from the first step to the last, even if things begin to go wrong—again.

Every day in parenting is a new day, a new beginning, a new chance to enjoy our children. Tomorrow, we can do it better.

Each day is a new day with God, too. We can focus on the things that matter most: worshipping Him, listening to Him, and being in His presence. No matter what happened the day before, we have a fresh start to enjoy a deeper relationship with Him.

Before I get out of bed in the morning, let me say these words and mean them: "This is the day the LORD has made; let us rejoice and be glad in it" (Psalm 118:24 NIV).

From Badlands to Glad Lands

I will restore to you the years that the locust hath eaten.

JOEL 2:25 KJV

Have you ever tilled a garden in the spring, breathing the earthy fragrance as sharp blades turned the moist, rich dirt? Perhaps you planted seeds and envisioned fresh vegetables. Or maybe you and your children have patted soil around tomato plants that promise a tasty harvest. Everyone loves flowers; we may get carried away with circus-colored visions of zinnias, marigolds, and petunias.

Then Japanese beetles and green worms discover our gardens and destroy our dreams. They bore holes and riddle leaves until our seed-catalog-perfect scene succumbs to their greedy appetites.

When God sent fierce enemies to punish their willful wrongdoing, the Israelites felt as if giant locusts had wiped out years of their lives. But God still loved them. He even promised to restore the years they lost because of their sin.

When we make bad choices, it's hard to believe anything good can grow in our lives again. But when God plants His seeds and rains His love down on us, we can expect the best!

Lord Jesus, I have not cultivated my life according to Your direc-tions. But You, the Resurrection and the Life, can bring spring-time to me today and every day. Thank You, Lord, for raining Your blessings upon me.

This, Too, Shall Pass

Weeping may endure for a night,
but joy comes in the morning.

PSALM 30:5 AMP

There may be night feedings that destroy your sleep. Terrible twos that seem never ending. No money for dinner and a movie. Trouble paying the electric bill. Rebellious teens. Disagreements with your spouse. Loneliness, discouragement, physical aches and pains. Being a mom can be downright tough.

But you know what? Every season has one thing in common—each has a beginning and an end. As with the calendar seasons of spring, summer, autumn, and winter, these "seasons" of your life will pass, too. By God's great design, no season lasts forever. No trial goes on endlessly.

The psalmist eloquently reminds us, "Weeping may endure for a night, but joy comes in the morning." He's not saying that if we can just hang on until sunrise, life will come up roses. The psalm writer is revealing that, though we may go through difficult trials, we can look forward with joy to the certainty of a new day. A new season of life. This, too, shall pass.

Heavenly Father, I often feel as if this season will never end.
Thank You for the hope of a new beginning—a new season of life.

Full of Hope

*Thy servant my husband is dead; and thou knowest
that thy servant did fear the LORD: and the creditor
is come to take unto him my two sons to be bondmen.*

2 KINGS 4:1 KJV

The woman had always supported her husband's studies with Elisha the prophet. But when her husband died suddenly and a creditor threatened to take her children as slaves, she fell at Elisha's feet, weeping.

"My husband loved God!" she cried. "But he is dead. We cannot pay our debts, and I may lose my sons! I have nothing but a pot of oil in the house."

"Borrow pots from your neighbors." His eyes held hers. "Then shut your door and pour oil into them."

After she had borrowed every pot on the block, she took her one pot of oil and began to pour. . .and pour. . .until all the pots were filled to the brim. Dizzy with excitement, she ran to Elisha.

He smiled as if expecting her. "Sell the oil to pay your debt; you and your children can live on the rest."

The widow ran home, thanking God from the bottom of her heart.

*Loving Lord, You provided for a mother with no hope for her
children. I know You can still do it today.*

Faithful One

Let us hold unswervingly to the hope we profess, for he who promised is faithful. And let us consider how we may spur one another on toward love and good deeds.

HEBREWS 10:23–24 NIV

When we have painful questions, therapists and counselors often have answers. But the people who offer the most practical and beneficial advice are those who have walked in our shoes.

Such people have helped us—and we, in turn, can help others. We may feel as if we have nothing to offer, but that's simply not so. As moms who have traveled the potholed road of parenthood, we can be a blessing to others who are just beginning the journey.

By holding tightly to the hope we have, we can benefit those around us who are struggling to find hope of their own. We can spur another hurting mom on to love and goodness and, in so doing, help ourselves better understand the God in whom our hope lies.

Dear Jesus, I know You are faithful—but I often forget that. Please forgive me, and help me to hold tighter to that which I know is true. Show me how to spur others toward Your love tomorrow.

[Your children] may forget what you said, but they will never forget how you made them feel.

CARL W. BUECHNER

By the River

"Blessed are those who trust in the LORD and have made the LORD their hope and confidence. They are like trees planted along a riverbank, with roots that reach deep into the water."

JEREMIAH 17:7–8 NLT

Trees lining a riverbank are often strange. They're twisted and gnarled, growing out of rocks or up through other trees. Though not always beautiful, these trees are strong and well nourished. With water always available, their roots plunge deeper than most other trees—strengthening their firm foundation, making their foliage brighter. Even their smell tends to be more refreshing than the rest.

God's Word says that if we put our trust and confidence in the Lord, allowing our hope to rest in His hands, we'll be like those strong, healthy trees. With our roots deep in the Lord, our foundation is firm and unshakable, our fruit brilliant and refreshing. We'll breathe in the fragrance of our Savior, drink in the river of life, and be strong and confident whatever may come.

Jesus, I thank You for Your faithfulness and ask that You'll help me to increase my trust and hope in You. Like those strong trees by the water's edge, may my roots go deep into Your Word, drinking from the river of life that never runs dry.

Best Paycheck

*"The LORD repay your work, and a full reward be
given you by the LORD God of Israel."*

RUTH 2:12 NKJV

Stepping back, the woman reviewed the kitchen she had
finished cleaning. Everything was spotless, but her shoulders slumped as she noted the rain and mud outside. Before
long her immaculate room would need cleaning once again.

Many jobs have to be done over and over, and they
become tedious and repetitive—dishes, laundry, vacuuming,
dusting. We want to complain about our drudgery, but we
don't stop to consider how God has given us these chores to
teach and perfect us.

Every day, all day, He is there to listen to our needs, to
answer prayers over and over. He never complains. He never
thinks we aren't worth His effort. He loves being there and
providing for us.

Sometimes the labor God gives us is new and exciting.
Sometimes the job is repetitive. Both types are given to us
for His purpose. We can look forward to the reward God
has for us when we complete the tasks He has set before us.

*Thank You, Lord, for the work I can do.
Give me joy and hope as I serve. Amen.*

Least Likely to Succeed

I will pour out my spirit upon all flesh;
and your sons and your daughters shall prophesy.

JOEL 2:28 KJV

Fourteen-year-old Noah poised drumsticks like weapons, ready to inflict noise on the congregation. His mother breathed the prayer that ruled her life: *Please, God, don't let him get carried away.*

Lisa adored her lovable son, yet Noah drove her—and everyone else—crazy. Now Lisa wished Noah were beside her, even if he fidgeted as if he were sitting on an anthill. But the youth pastor thought playing drums during the service might focus Noah's energy in a positive direction.

Instead Noah smacked the drums and smashed the cymbals until Lisa's head throbbed. How could anybody find that much rhythm in "What a Friend We Have in Jesus"? Afterward Lisa tried to hurry Noah out the church door.

"I *love* to hear a young man praise God with enthusiasm!" said old Mrs. Richards, blocking their escape. "He's using you, Noah!"

Lisa's son never did learn to sit still in church. But ten years later, as Noah worked in an inner-city center, winning teens to Christ, he didn't have to.

Open my eyes, Lord, and help me see Jesus
working in my children today.

Christmas Comes on Leaden Feet

A day is like a thousand years to the Lord, and a thousand years is like a day. The Lord isn't really being slow about his promise, as some people think. No, he is being patient for your sake. He does not want anyone to be destroyed, but wants everyone to repent.

2 PETER 3:8–9 NLT

To a child, December 25 takes forever to arrive!

But to a mom, Christmas comes altogether too quickly. It's exactly the same amount of time—but different viewpoints lead to very different perceptions.

In the first-century church, believers were growing impatient. Jesus had promised to return—but where was He? Like children waiting for Christmas, the early believers couldn't experience Jesus' second coming quickly enough.

God, though, sees time differently than we do. In His love and wisdom, He's giving time to everyone to repent from their sins and truly know Him. His agenda, unlike ours, is always perfectly holy.

Though it may seem like Jesus will never return, the Bible promises He will come, and our long wait will one day be forgotten.

It will be a Christmas morning that lasts forever!

Lord of the universe, You are coming back! May I model patience and expectancy to my family, never wavering in my belief that You will return!

Establishing a Vision

Where there is no vision, the people perish.

<small>PROVERBS 29:18 KJV</small>

Cookbooks without pictures aren't much fun. Simple words on a page typically don't move us to culinary pursuits. But if that decadent New York–style cheesecake recipe is actually pictured, we may *run* to the kitchen!

Moms, too, need an image of what we're trying to accomplish. What do we see as the end result of all our efforts? What does success in our family, our parenting, our career, our spiritual life look like? We need a vision. Without it we'll probably walk aimlessly through piles of laundry, stacks of bills, and grocery store aisles.

With a clear mental image of the future, we can visualize where all the hard work of parenthood is taking us—and see, in our mind's eye, the big picture of what God is creating in us and in the lives of our children.

Ask God to give you a vision of your ultimate destination. It'll make worlds of difference in your day-to-day labors.

Father God, allow me to see the vision You have established for my family—embed it into my heart and mind.

Nothing you do for children is ever wasted.
They seem not to notice us, hovering, averting our
eyes, and they seldom offer thanks, but what
we do for them is never wasted.

GARRISON KEILLOR

Comfort

The Gift

Sons are a heritage from the LORD, children a reward from him.
Like arrows in the hands of a warrior are sons born in one's youth.
Blessed is the man whose quiver is full of them.

PSALM 127:3–5 NIV

"Sit down and be quiet for five minutes! Give me a minute's peace!"

Sound familiar?

Children are demanding, loud, selfish, and messy. That's not new. When they're young, they need diaper changes, naps, blankies, and, most importantly, *Mommy*. As they get older, they need help with homework, transportation everywhere, lunch money, and, a bit less importantly, *Mom*.

Children are a bunch of fun and endless work—and no matter how big they get, they are forever our babies. Through our children, God says, we are blessed. Our little ones are a reward from Him!

If you have children, you are blessed—and the more you have, the more blessed you are. Try to remember that the next time you hear "Mommy. . .I need you!"

Lord, I thank You for my precious children. I often get frustrated and forget they are gifts from You. Help me to remember they are a blessing—and my life would be incomplete without them. Thank You for blessing me with such an irreplaceable gift.

Walk and Pray

*And pray in the Spirit on all occasions with all kinds of prayers
and requests. With this in mind, be alert and always keep on
praying for all the saints.*

EPHESIANS 6:18 NIV

Their friendship began when their daughters played on the
same soccer team. They soon realized after a couple of conversations that they had more in common than two ener-
getic thirteen-year-old girls. They shared a common faith in
God, and both women were experiencing the growing pains
that come with parenting adolescents.

One day the women decided to start wearing their
workout gear to practice so that they could talk and pray for
their daughters as they walked the perimeter of the soccer
field. By the end of the season both women were encouraged
and strengthened, and they had forged a deep friendship.

Jesus said, "For where two or three come together in
my name, there am I with them" (Matthew 18:20 NIV). Real
power is available when friends get together for fellowship
and prayer, because Christ Himself is right there with them.

Is there a friend you might call today to join you in a
prayer walk?

*Heavenly Father, thank You for faithful friends, and thank You
for Jesus, the most faithful friend of all. Amen.*

Eat Your Fill

There is a time for everything, and a season for every activity
under heaven. . .a time to embrace and a time to refrain.

ECCLESIASTES 3:1, 5 NIV

Author Carol Kuykendall tells a story of stopping at a road-side fruit stand after dropping her son off at college. As she filled a bag with peaches, the cashier commented, "Better eat your fill of those peaches. When they're gone, you won't miss them so much."

Carol felt the cashier had given her wisdom that applied to more than peaches. She went home, cleared her calendar of all but necessities for the year and became more available for her daughter still living at home.

When her daughter left for college, they were closer than ever, and she wasn't burdened by regret over missed moments.

Wise old Solomon observed a certain pattern that God Himself had set into motion: seasons of nature, seasons of change in our lives. Solomon could see the big picture, understanding that we have little control over many things. Instead of fighting that rhythm, we can embrace it, acknowledging that seasons are part of God's plan for our lives.

Lord, help us to see our lives with a long view.
Give us Your peace as we face our future,
knowing You are in control.

One Home Run
after Another

But Daniel resolved not to defile himself.

DANIEL 1:8 NIV

Whenever Daniel came to bat, he never missed! He hit a home run off every pitch thrown to him: The fastballs, like Daniel's guilt-by-association death sentence when Nebuchadnezzar demanded the killing of all wise men because they could not interpret the king's dream; the curveballs, like the one Daniel's jealous colleagues threw to him when they tricked the king into making a law that sent people to the lion's den for bowing and praying to anyone but the king. Did that prevent Daniel from praying to God? No. Not our star player.

If only we had a batting record like Daniel's. Parenting is hard for us. Sometimes we foul out. At other times, we just watch the pitches whiz by. We strike out a lot.

What made Daniel a home run hitter? He sought God's wisdom and discernment, and he had a habit of prayer. He knew that God—not some earthly king—was in control of this world.

We may not be home run hitters, but we can improve our batting average—by resolving to love God wholeheartedly.

Lord, I pray that each member of my household will be like Daniel—loving You devotedly and with his or her whole being.

The successful mother, the mother who does her part in rearing and training aright the boys and girls who are to be the men and women of the next generation, is of greater use to the community. . . . She is more important by far than the successful statesman or businessman or artist or scientist.

THEODORE ROOSEVELT

My Steps

*"His eyes are on the ways of men;
he sees their every step."*

JOB 34:21 NIV

Tammy watched her son intently. She had been teaching him for the past month not to walk into the street without her. It had been a daunting lesson, but Tammy felt it was extremely valuable.

Today Josh stood on the sidewalk, arms stretched toward his favorite ball that had rolled into the street. Tammy's eyes were glued to her son, watching for any quick movement toward the dangerous street. She held her breath and moved within arm's reach, lest he step out to retrieve his toy.

Life can sometimes feel as though *we* are wandering onto a busy street with dangerous traffic zipping all around. But all the while, God keeps His eyes on us, and when we do stumble, He is always within arm's reach—ready to catch us, love us, and teach us once again His perfect ways.

Father, I may not know what direction my life will take or where my path may lead. I do know, though, that You never take Your eyes off me, guiding me and catching me when I stumble. Thank You for loving me so much.

One Day at a Time

Blessed be the Lord, who daily loadeth us with benefits,
even the God of our salvation.

PSALM 68:19 KJV

There's a reason why the Lord's Prayer teaches us to ask for daily bread. God calls us to a childlike faith, one that basks in the provisions of the moment and forgets yesterday's disappointments and tomorrow's worries.

Think about small children. A toddler may cry when another child knocks him down and takes away his ball. The tears disappear when his mother hugs him and gives him a kiss. Later he returns to the ball with fresh enthusiasm. He lives in the moment.

God always provides for us. Benefits overflow the shopping carts of our lives every single day. But He only gives us what we need for today, not for tomorrow. He knows that we need those benefits like a daily vitamin.

By this evening we may forget all that God has done for us, but God gives us blessings every day so that we still have what we need after we have spent ourselves on life's disappointments.

Father, You give us bread daily. We praise You for Your
constant care and ask that You will train our eyes to
focus on Your blessings, not on our failings. Amen.

Help for the Tough Times

"I will not leave you as orphans; I will come to you."

JOHN 14:18 NIV

Joan stared at the envelope in her hand. Another wedding invitation, this time from her cousin's daughter. She set it aside, annoyed that it made her feel so alone.

Joan knew all too well that she was *not* alone. Her days were filled with work, church commitments, and the buzz of her two teenagers in and out of the house. Friends frequently dropped by, and sometimes her days were nonstop from dawn to bedtime, leaving her barely enough time to breathe.

Yet the loneliness created by her husband's death never quite left her, no matter how active her life. There were times Joan struggled to move on to the next task when all she wanted to do was grieve. Only when she remembered God's promise to always be there did she feel any relief.

God never, ever abandons us no matter how busy we are. He promised His followers that He would always help and support them, a promise He still keeps today.

Lord, You sent Your Holy Spirit as a helper and guide.
No matter how tough our world becomes, let us remember
Your presence in our lives. Amen.

Because I Love You. . .

"Because he loves me," says the LORD, "I will rescue him;
I will protect him, for he acknowledges my name."

PSALM 91:14 NIV

A brother and sister were arguing over the last piece of pizza. That's when Mom saved the day by revealing a second "last" piece.

"Where did that come from?" one of the children asked.

"I'd held this one out as my dinner," the mom answered.

Puzzled, the other child asked, "Why would you do that? Then you won't have *any* dinner."

"Because I love you, sweetheart. Now you can both have another slice—go ahead and enjoy it."

Scenes like this are replayed countless times by countless mothers all over the world. Why? Because we love our kids. Plain and simple.

God wants us to love Him, too, and He reminds us in the psalms that He will protect and rescue those who love and acknowledge Him. Our love for Him is a key that opens the door of His provisions. It's not our accomplishment or achievement that God wants—He longs for us to love Him.

Father, if I love my children sacrificially, how much more do
You care for me? Wow! I love You, Lord.

Janitor or Judge

The Lord says this to you:
Be not afraid or dismayed at this great multitude;
for the battle is not yours, but God's.

2 CHRONICLES 20:15 AMP

Wanting what's best for our children is what drives us, really. We push them to excel academically. We fret over their vitamin intake and how to discipline them properly. And why not? Their future rests in our hands.

Though we very much want our kids to have a good life without any financial or social strife, that particular objective may be a bit shortsighted. Will those things bring genuine happiness and contentment? Haven't we all seen celebrities who "have everything" yet are riddled with discontent and depression?

Our highest aim is to raise children who genuinely love God and want to serve Him. And they can do that whether they become judges or janitors, press operators or presidents.

God is the only One worthy of our kids' devotion, and the only One able to lead and guide them through this life. The battle is His, not ours—so trust Him with your family.

Father, what a relief to know I don't fight this battle alone. I've felt
such pressure to be the "perfect" parent. I acknowledge my need
for Your guidance and wisdom as I raise my children.

When God thought of mother, He must have laughed with satisfaction, and framed it quickly— so rich, so deep, so divine, so full of soul, power, and beauty, was the conception.

HENRY WARD BEECHER

The House of Babel

"Let Us go down there and confuse their language so that they will not understand one another's speech." So the LORD scattered them from there over the face of the whole earth, and they stopped building the city. Therefore its name is called Babylon.

GENESIS 11:7–9 HCSB

Early in biblical history the world's people spoke only one language. They wandered about, came to a plain in Babylonia, and settled there. Then they decided to build a tower, a religious symbol, to reach the sky. On top of this tower there was probably an altar on which human sacrifices were offered. In punishment, God responded by confounding their language.

Communication is a powerful tool. But it's often confounded, even in our homes. There are times when parents seem to speak a totally different language from their children! Thankfully God can cut through all the miscommunication. He hears and understands what we're saying, and He speaks to us, too. God says, "I will instruct you and show you the way to go; . . . I will give counsel" (Psalm 32:8 HCSB). But that requires listening as much as talking.

Lord, unstuff my ears and those of my children!
Help us to listen carefully to Your voice and to each other.

Beautiful Scars

*"The Spirit of the LORD is upon Me, because He has. . .
sent Me to heal the brokenhearted."*

LUKE 4:18 NKJV

We all have physical scars, and each tells its own story. Some of those tales might be humorous, but others conjure darker memories. Scars are caused by what has either been done to us or through us.

The most painful scars are often those that others can't see. They are the silent wounds on our hearts—the scar of rejection from an unloving father, the scar of disappointment at the loss of a child, the scar of a broken marriage—all painful reminders of the imperfect, fallen world we live in.

Whatever their cause, those injuries present us an opportunity. They are an invitation for us to share in the healing power of Jesus Christ. He can heal our open wounds and smooth over the tough, unsightly scars on our souls.

Painful memories may remain, but after we experience Jesus' healing touch, our scars can tell of His goodness. He can use even our scars for His glory.

*Thank You, Lord, for Your healing power. Please help me to
reveal my scars so that You can use the pain of my
wounds to reach others with Your love.*

Sudden Disasters

*We take captive every thought
to make it obedient to Christ.*

2 Corinthians 10:5 niv

Sandra hadn't heard from her son, a freshman in college, for two weeks. Her thoughts raced with worry. *Maybe he's sick or he's been injured. Maybe he doesn't have his wallet with him and is languishing in a hospital bed, listed as John Doe. What if he's flunking out of college and doesn't want to tell me?*

Moms are very good at worrying. Most of us can go from zero to sixty in under four seconds with catastrophic thinking, especially if we're worried about our kids.

What does scripture tell us about those what-if worries? Scripture tells us to "have no fear of sudden disaster or of the ruin that overtakes the wicked, for the LORD will be your confidence and will keep your foot from being snared" (Proverbs 3:25–26 niv).

What? No fear of sudden disaster? No fear, God says. Even when we wake in the night with a troubling thought? No fear. Even the first time our child drives off with a brand-new driver's license in his wallet? Even then. No fear—for the Lord is our confidence as we capture each thought.

*Lord God, take my thoughts—every thought—
and renew them with Your Word.*

A Labor of Love

*Therefore, my beloved brethren, be firm (steadfast), immovable. . .
knowing and being continually aware that your labor in the
Lord is not futile [it is never wasted or to no purpose].*

1 CORINTHIANS 15:58 AMP

"Cover your mouth!"

"Did you brush your teeth?"

"Don't talk with your mouth full!"

"No, you can*not* eat candy for breakfast."

To the casual observer, it may appear that our labor of love—with all of its dos, don'ts, and did yous—has been for naught. After all, how many times should one have to say, "Don't kick your sister!" before Bobby finally gets it? Apparently ninety-eight and counting.

And then there are the deeper issues of life. We teach our kids to treat mean people with kindness, to forgive when they would rather hold a grudge. They're hard lessons to learn, but our labor is not in vain. We have His Word on it.

Raising children to love and honor the Lord is tough work, but the key is never to give in to discouragement. Nothing we do for the Lord is ever wasted. . .even reminding little Bobby to stop kicking his sister!

*Father God, as I raise my children to honor and respect
You, You've promised that my labor is never wasted.
What a promise to count on!*

Beauty of the Beholder

*So God created human beings in his own image. In the image of
God he created them; male and female he created them. . . . Then
God looked over all he had made, and he saw that it was very good!*

GENESIS 1:27, 31 NLT

Janet looked in the mirror and winced. *I shouldn't have eaten
that extra piece of cake,* she thought as she pinched a bit of fat
around her waist.

Many women tend to find something wrong with
themselves, no matter how they actually look. Though
there's nothing wrong with presenting ourselves in the best
light, we should always remember one important fact: God
created us in His image. The One who created us loves us
exactly as we are!

Those little things we see as imperfections are actually
attractive to God. Just as we see our own kids as the most
adorable things, God sees us as His lovely children. When it
comes to self-image, let's try to see ourselves through God's
eyes, remembering that His creation is always good.

*Dear Lord, when I look in the mirror, remind me that I was
created in Your image and that, although I may not always
see myself as beautiful, You think I look very good.*

Where we love is home—home that our feet may leave but not our hearts.

OLIVER WENDELL HOLMES SR.

Rest

In His Arms

I will both lay me down in peace, and sleep:
for thou, LORD, only makest me dwell in safety.

PSALM 4:8 KJV

Sally read until her eyes could no longer stay open. She closed her book, shut off the light, and let her head sink into the comfort of her pillow.

As her eyes closed, Sally's mind began to roam free. *Will seven hours be enough sleep tonight? I didn't get nearly enough done today. . . . I wonder if my car will pass inspection next month. We can't afford a new one. . . .*

Sally shook her head. Frustrated at the turn of her thoughts, she rose and reached for her Bible. Sally opened up to a favorite verse—Psalm 4:8: "Lay me down in peace, and sleep. . .makest me dwell in safety." She smiled, letting God's Word saturate her mind. Then she fell asleep, cradled in His arms.

Don't let futile worries keep you from catching those forty winks. Fall asleep in God's Word, rest easy, and rise refreshed.

God, with Your Word in my thoughts, I can lie down in peace and sleep. You will keep me safe, now and forever, as I rest and then rise in Your power. Amen.

A Little Time with God

"I thank You and praise You, O God of my fathers;
You have given me wisdom and might."

DANIEL 2:23 NKJV

Susan headed out of her house in the same way she always did—in a hurry, double-checking her children's backpacks as she went and reminding them of chores and practices scheduled for that afternoon. "Remember, 3:30 is ballet; 4:00 is soccer. I'll pick you up after school, but I have to go back to work, so—"

She stopped as her coat snagged on a bush. As she stooped to untangle the cloth, the stem bent suddenly, and Susan found herself nose to petal with a rose. It smelled glorious, and she paused, laughing.

Susan glanced up toward the sky. "Thanks for grabbing me. I guess I should spend a little more time with You."

God blesses us every day in both great and simple ways. Children, friends, work, faith—all these things form a bountiful buffet of gifts, and caring for them isn't always enough. We need to spend a little time with the One who has granted us the blessings.

Father God, You have given us so much to be grateful for.
Show me a way to spend more time with You, and help me
to grow closer and know You better. Amen.

One Thing Is Needed

"Martha, Martha," the Lord answered, "you are worried and upset about many things, but only one thing is needed."

LUKE 10:41–42 NIV

We are each given twenty-four hours in a day. Einstein and Edison were given no more than Joseph and Jeremiah of the Old Testament. Even Mother Teresa and plain ol' moms are peers when it comes to time.

Time—we can't buy it, save it, or get a greater share, no matter what we do. So we should learn to use it carefully. Do we tackle the laundry now or help the kids read their favorite book one more time? Do we fuss over our hair and makeup or find a moment to kneel before our Father?

Since God has blessed each of us with twenty-four hours, let's seek His direction on how to spend this invaluable commodity wisely—spending more time on relationships than the rat race. In Luke, our Lord reminded dear, dogged, drained Martha that only one thing is needed—Him.

Father God, oftentimes I get caught up in the minutiae of life. The piled laundry can appear more important than the precious little ones You've given me. Help me to use my time wisely. Open my eyes to see what is truly important.

Creating a Margin

*"My Presence will go with you,
and I will give you rest."*

EXODUS 33:14 NIV

From the very first chapter of Genesis, God teaches us to take rest. He rested on the seventh day of creation and declared it good. Later, as the Israelites entered the Promised Land, God ordered the people to give the *soil* a rest every seven years.

When we short ourselves on rest, illness can result. That's our body's way of saying "Slow down! I can't keep up! If you won't listen to me, then I'm going to force you to."

God believes in rest! But most of us live lives that are packed to the brim with activities and obligations. We're overwhelmed. With such a fragile balance, unexpected occurrences, like a dead car battery, can wreck us emotionally, spiritually, and physically.

That's not the lifestyle God wants us to have. "He grants sleep to those he loves," wrote the psalmist (Psalm 127:2 NIV). God wants us to create a margin for the unexpected: a neighbor in need, a grandparent who requires extra attention, a friend who needs encouragement, our own kids as they grow and mature.

Life is busy. But in God's presence we find rest.

*Help me, Father, to listen to Your
instruction and heed Your words.*

Sleep on It

It is of the LORD's mercies that we are not consumed, because his compassions fail not. They are new every morning: great is thy faithfulness.

LAMENTATIONS 3:22–23 KJV

"Sleep on it." Researchers have found that to be sound advice. They believe that sleep helps people sort through facts, thoughts, and memories, providing a clearer look at the big picture upon waking. Sleep also separates reality from emotions like fear and worry, which can cloud our thinking and interfere with rational decision making. Scientifically speaking, sleep is good medicine.

For Christians the biological effects of sleep are outweighed by the spiritual benefits of the new day God gives us. At the end of an exhausting day, after the worries and the pressures of life have piled high, we may lie down, feeling as though we can't take another moment of stress. But God's Word tells us that His great mercy will keep our worries and problems from consuming us.

Through the never-ending compassion of God, we can eagerly anticipate the new day, leaving behind the concerns of yesterday.

Heavenly Father, thank You for giving me a new measure of Your mercy and compassion each day so that my concerns don't consume me. I rest in You, and I lay my burdens at Your feet.

*Give a little love to a child, and
you get a great deal back.*

JOHN RUSKIN

How About Some Fun?

A twinkle in the eye means joy in the heart,
and good news makes you feel fit as a fiddle.

PROVERBS 15:30 MSG

"Have you had any fun this week?"

This query, in and of itself, might sound odd, but God does not want His kids to be worn down and stressed out. He did not design us to be like little Energizer Bunnies that keep on going and going and going. We need time to *recreate*—to revive and refresh our bodies and minds. A little relaxation, recreation—and, yes—*fun* are essential components of a balanced life. Even Jesus and His disciples found it necessary to get away from the crowds and pressures of ministry to rest.

There's a lot of fun to be had out there—playing tennis or golf, jogging, swimming, painting, knitting, playing a musical instrument, visiting an art gallery, playing a board game, or going to a movie, a play, or a football game. How will you have fun this week?

Lord, You are the One who gives balance to my life. Help me to find time today for a little relaxation, recreation, and even fun.
Amen.

A Day of Rest

Six days thou shalt do thy work, and on the seventh day thou shalt rest: that thine ox and thine ass may rest, and the son of thy handmaid, and the stranger, may be refreshed.

EXODUS 23:12 KJV

If there is one scriptural principle that women routinely abandon, it is that of the Sabbath. Because Christ has become our rest and because we now worship on the Lord's Day, we often disregard the idea of a Sabbath rest.

Rest was at the heart of the Sabbath. One day out of seven, God's people were not to work or to make others work, so they could all be refreshed.

God Himself started the work-rest pattern before the earth was a week old. God didn't rest because He was tired; He rested because His work of creation was finished.

But a woman's work is never done! How can she rest?

It's not easy. There are always more things that can be done. But most of those things can wait a day while you recharge.

God's design for the week gives rest to the weary. Let's not neglect His provision.

Father, help me to rest from my labor as You rested from Yours. Refresh me this day. Amen.

Time Is Fleeting

Teach us to realize the brevity of life,
so that we may grow in wisdom.

PSALM 90:12 NLT

....

"They grow up so fast."

We've all heard it, probably even said it ourselves. It's oft repeated because it's so true. Our children's childhood is fleeting. Our opportunity to influence them is moving at breakneck speed. Yet many of us are so absorbed in day-to-day parenting that we don't recognize that time is escaping quickly.

We rush little Johnny to school. Hurry little Sarah to day care. Speed through the workweek to spend Saturday and Sunday doing extra chores around the house. Maybe we'll occasionally take a week's vacation just to catch our breath. But then we're off to the races again.

What if we determined to enjoy the moment? To savor the innocence of our child's kindergarten graduation performance? Maybe we should sit back and really listen to our teenage daughter as she describes her favorite band. Perhaps we could enjoy a Saturday morning breakfast of cold pizza with the kids—in our pajamas.

Life is brief. So is our opportunity to influence our children.

Father, help me to see how fleeting is the
time with the little ones You've given me.
And please help me make the most of that time.

Want Rest? Invest!

Correct thy son, and he shall give thee rest; yea,
he shall give delight unto thy soul.

PROVERBS 29:17 KJV

The house was tidy, orderly, and quiet.

Outside, as the breezes blew, the mother of the house relaxed on a lounge chair, visiting with a friend. Inside, her six children were napping or occupied with quiet activities.

"I need this time to rest," the mother explained, "so I can recharge my battery."

And the children let her rest.

How had this happened?

This mother had learned the secret of child rearing. She had lovingly trained her children consistently from their arrival. Her babies' meals, naps, and playtimes were carefully scheduled. She gave her older children responsibilities in the form of chores, always on hand to look over their work and give them correction and encouragement when needed.

Taking the time to consistently train our children isn't always easy in the given moment, but such an investment in our time will return peace and joy to the house.

Father, being a mother day in and day out is hard work.
Yet I know my children are a good investment of my time
and love. Thank You for giving me opportunities to
rest in the fruit of this labor. Amen.

No Time

It is good to give thanks to the LORD, to sing praises to the Most High. It is good to proclaim your unfailing love in the morning, your faithfulness in the evening.

PSALM 92:1–2 NLT

Two mothers waited in line at the grocery store. Sharon looked tired and complained about not having enough time in her day. Her four-year-old son was fussing and whining sleepily. Lisa listened with sympathy.

"What am I doing wrong?" Sharon asked.

Lisa took a deep breath and responded, "Did you spend time with the Lord this morning?"

Sharon admitted she hadn't.

"Spending time with the Lord makes my day run more smoothly." Lisa could tell Sharon wasn't completely satisfied, and she said a little prayer for her as they parted.

A few weeks later the two women ran into each other again. Sharon and her child looked more peaceful and rested. "Lisa, thank you so much for reminding me to spend time with the Lord. It has changed my life. Not only do I have time to get everything done, but I have time for the Lord in the evenings as well."

Heavenly Father, it is my desire to grow closer to You. Help me to remember to spend time with You each day—no matter how busy I am. Amen.

When we do the best that we can,
we never know what miracle is wrought
in our life or in the life of another.

HELEN KELLER

Rest and Restore

*"Come to me, all you who are weary and burdened,
and I will give you rest."*

MATTHEW 11:28 NIV

Weary and burdened—such is the daily existence of a mom.
Weary from long hours of working, cleaning, and parenting—
giving all we have to our children. Burdened from knowing
we have to do it all again tomorrow and the next day and the
day after that.

Thankfully we don't have to stay in this exhausting
place. God offers rest to the mom whose shoulders are tired
from carrying much more than her share of burdens. "Come
to Me," says the Lord. "I want to give you rest."

When we bring Him our weary spirits, He replaces our
burdens with His comfortable rest. He gives us strength to
get through tomorrow and the next day and the day after
that.

When we continually go to the Lord for rest, we'll find
that, even though our situations don't change, we can get
through our days with peace rather than exhaustion.

*Lord God, You are the Giver of rest. I come to You in faith,
putting my heavy load in Your hands. I ask You to replace
it with Your sweet rest, restoring my spirit, body,
and mind for this journey.*

Treading Water

With the crowd dispersed, he climbed the mountain so he could be by himself and pray. He stayed there alone, late into the night.

MATTHEW 14:23 MSG

Treading water is not a sign of weakness. It's a tactic swimmers employ before their strength begins to fail. When weariness comes on, the swimmer stops pulling herself through the water, instead gently moving her arms and legs ever so slightly to remain above water. No progress is made while treading water, but time is gained for strength to recover.

Moms often feel like they're drowning—losing strength as the waters overtake them. So "treading water" for a time may be the best choice. We won't make any great advancements during that time—but a conscious decision to take no large steps, address no big issues, and simply rest can be exactly what we need to regroup.

Tread water for a few days, even weeks, if necessary. Reconnect with God through prayer and introspection. Let the Holy Spirit renew your soul and body so you can begin the journey once again with a new vigor.

Jesus, please renew and reenergize me as a parent and as a believer. Through rest and prayer, please strengthen me and return me to the vigor I once felt.

Elbow Grease

*It is useless for you to work so hard from early
morning until late at night, anxiously working for
food to eat; for God gives rest to his loved ones.*

PSALM 127:2 NLT

Take it easy! Relax. Don't sweat the small stuff. Life is short.
Stop and smell the roses. Yeah, you've heard it all before, but
there's just no way to carve out time for some good old rest
and relaxation.

Who'll cook dinner if you don't? How will the kids get
to their after-school activities if you don't take them? And
yes, midnight is a bit late to be folding laundry—but it has
to be done, doesn't it?

Of course those things must be done, and the duties
usually do fall to us moms. But would it really be the end of
the world if your daughter wore the same pair of jeans twice
in a row or everyone ate leftovers for dinner?

What *would* be regretful is if you stayed up late every
night and continually got up at the crack of dawn, only to
find yourself burned-out and angry—even physically sick.
God calls this overeffort "useless." Do what needs to be
done and then relax. Take Him up on His offer of rest!

*Father God, I am tired of working so hard and feeling so empty.
Please enable me simply to relax.*

The Ant's Lesson

Go to the ant, O sluggard; consider her ways, and be wise. . . .
She prepares her bread in summer and gathers her food in harvest.

PROVERBS 6:6, 8 ESV

Moms treasure Saturday mornings. We don't have to rush anywhere. We can catch a little extra sleep and spend a quiet, contented morning (we hope) at home.

Those times to rest and recharge are necessary. But problems can start when we set our alarm later and later each weekend then hit our SNOOZE button once or twice or more. *No, really—just five minutes more.*

In contrast, Solomon points us to the example of the lowly ant. Think of what that tiny bug accomplishes: She locates food and carries home as much as she can manage. She makes a note of where the rest of the food is located. She stays busy and is always prepared.

What might we accomplish in an extra five, ten, or fifteen minutes a day? Has our quiet time slid by the wayside? Is there a stack of mail needing our attention? Can we play a game with our children or read a book together?

Let's consider the ant's ways and be wise!

Lord, teach me the balance between necessary rest and laziness.
Teach me to use my time wisely.

Finding Real Rest

And I said, Oh that I had wings like a dove!
for then would I fly away, and be at rest.

PSALM 55:6 KJV

There are days. . .
 when the family gets sick and the dog disappears,
 when the phone doesn't stop ringing,
 when your boss takes his frustration out on you,
 when you think things can't get any worse, but they do.
 There are days.

 Sometimes it's tempting to wish you could get away from all the people who want more than you have to give.

 If only you could fly away! Then you could be at rest.

 Really?

 Often, even if we go away from the noise and demands of family, we find ourselves thinking of the very ones we wanted to leave. Instead of being at peace, we're full of guilt and regret.

 Rather than fly away, we must jump into God's everlasting arms and dive into His Word. Rest is found in knowing Christ and understanding that through His sacrifice, we are at peace.

Father God, there are many days when I don't have time to sit.
And too often my house is Crisis Central. In all these times
remind me that peace comes from knowing You and resting
in the work You have done. Amen.

One of God's richest blessings…is that our children come into the world as people we're supposed to guide and direct, and then God uses them to form us—if we will only listen.

DENA DYER

God's Guidance

Money + Time = Achieved Goals

Easy come, easy go, but steady diligence pays off.
PROVERBS 13:11 MSG

When Julia's children were little, she lived in the Seattle area. She often read in the newspaper about a little computer company that seemed to be going somewhere. When the company went public, she bought ten shares of stock for each child—all she could afford to spend comfortably.

Julia let the stock sit. Sixteen years later Julia sold the stock. That small investment funded her children's college education.

God wants us to prepare for our future with wise planning. There are major costs ahead that we know we will be facing: orthodontics, college tuition, weddings. Planning for the future by saving diligently, combined with the benefit of time, will help us reach those goals.

Someone asked Julia if she wished she had bought more stock—that she had put everything she had into that company. But, she explained, it wasn't her intention to get rich quick. Her goal was simply to prepare for the funding of her children's college education—and the Lord blessed her efforts.

Lord, give me wisdom in how I spend my money and how I save my money. Bless my efforts to prepare for my children's future.

Say You're Sorry

"Don't tear your clothing in your grief, but tear your hearts instead. Return to the LORD your God."

JOEL 2:13 NLT

How many times in a week do moms tell their children, "Say you're sorry"? And how many times does the "sorry" come out sounding like anything but an apology? There's sorrow for sin, and then there's sorrow for getting caught in sin.

When God commands us to repent, He doesn't want a mumbled apology. He doesn't even want demonstrative tears—unless they come from a repentant heart. The scripture above from Joel shows true repentance. Repentance for sinning against God involves a willful action, a changing of direction. It's doing it God's way, going in God's direction. We can't always undo or fix all our wrong actions. But when it's in our power to do so, the Lord gives us specific guidelines. When we do our part, He does His because "he is merciful and compassionate" (Joel 2:13 NLT).

Forgive me, Lord, for my sin against You and others. Help me to right those things I can right and not to repeat the same errors. Amen.

All by Myself

*Thou say in thine heart, My power and the might of mine hand
hath gotten me this wealth. But thou shalt remember the LORD
thy God: for it is he that giveth thee power to get wealth.*

DEUTERONOMY 8:17–18 KJV

Little Logan set up a lemonade stand. He squeezed the
lemon slices his mom had cut into a pitcher of water and set
out the sign he'd made: ICE COLD LEMONADE—75¢.

At first only Mom came, but soon others arrived. Logan yelled, "Mommy, I'm rich! And I did it all by myself!"

Logan did not consider his mother's investment in his
supplies—or her time. It never crossed his mind that she
had tipped off his customers on the phone about the stand
while he waited for business to magically appear!

We smile at a little boy's self-centeredness, but sometimes we adults act that way, too. God showers us with
health, intelligence, education, and opportunity. Every breath
and heartbeat are gifts from Him! Like Logan we never
suspect the roles He plays behind the scenes to encourage
and prosper us.

*Father, please forgive me when I take credit for blessings You give
because of Your generous heart. Help me use them for Your glory.
Amen.*

Be a Wise Builder

Every wise woman buildeth her house:
but the foolish plucketh it down with her hands.

PROVERBS 14:1 KJV

No matter the season of her life, no matter what house she is in, a woman should be about the business of building a home and a family.

While home building is the highest calling of womanhood, we sometimes turn aside from it, thinking the world offers something better. We sometimes think the world's view of personal achievement is better than God's view of submission and self-sacrifice.

Don't be fooled—real wisdom is found as we apply scripture to the many tasks of homemaking. Teaching kindness to a two-year-old is more difficult than teaching economic theory to graduate students, and explaining salvation to a preschooler is more challenging than convincing a bank to finance a business plan.

When done well, home building will yield rewards for many generations. When done thoughtlessly, generations suffer.

Let's not neglect this great task for the Lord.

Let us be wise builders.

Father, even though I know building a home is my most important job, sometimes I don't see the value. Let me labor in my home with diligence and grace, knowing it is truly my best work. Amen.

The mother love is like God's love; He loves us not because we are lovable, but because it is His nature to love and because we are His children.

EARL RINEY

Can God Interrupt You?

In his heart a man plans his course,
but the LORD determines his steps.

PROVERBS 16:9 NIV

Before rushing out of the house each morning, we grab calendars or PalmPilots. Our day is efficiently planned. We are eager to check off our to-do list. But wait! The phone suddenly rings. There is an unexpected knock at the door. The car tire is flat.

How do we react when our plans are interrupted? Do frustration, resentment, and anger quickly surface?

Have you ever considered that perhaps God has ordained our interruptions? A friend could be calling in need of encouragement. Maybe the knock on the door is a lost child seeking help. Perhaps, just perhaps, God may be trying to get your attention.

There is nothing wrong with planning your day. However, be open. Be flexible. God sees the big picture. Allow Him to change your plans according to His will. Instead of becoming frustrated, look for ways the Lord might be working. When you do, interruptions will become blessings.

Dear Lord, forgive me when I am so rigidly locked into my own agenda that I miss Yours. Give me Your eternal perspective so that I may be open to divine interruptions. Amen.

Walk in the Light

*Then Jesus spoke to them again, saying, "I am the light
of the world. He who follows Me shall not walk
in darkness, but have the light of life."*

JOHN 8:12 NKJV

A woman and her family regularly vacationed on a secluded
island. They loved it because it was private and could be
reached only by boat.

One night the woman went for a walk without thinking
to take along a flashlight. She found her way easily along the
paths at first, but as the twilight waned, the trails became so
black that she was forced to stop. She listened to the sounds
around her as she stood, frozen, afraid to take another step.

At that moment she heard her daughter's voice and saw
a light bobbing down the sandy trail toward her. "Mom, you
forgot your flashlight; I was worried." How thankful she was
for the light that illuminated their way back to the cottage.

We can be thankful for the light that illuminates our
paths—the Word of God. Without it we would stumble
along through life, always unsure of our path.

*Heavenly Father, thank You for Your Word that is a
lamp unto my feet and a light to my path. Amen.*

Reflecting God in Our Work

Whatever you do, work at it with all your heart,
as working for the Lord, not for men.

COLOSSIANS 3:23 NIV

....

Children are a reflection of their parents. When a mom and
dad send their offspring out into the world, they can only
hope that the reflection will be a positive one.

As believers we are God's children. No one is perfect,
and for this there is grace. However, we may be the only
reflection of our heavenly Father that some will ever see.
Our attitudes and actions on the job speak volumes to those
around us. Although it may be tempting to do just enough
to get by, we put forth our best effort when we remember
we represent God to the world. A Christian's character on
the job should be a positive reflection of the Lord.

This is true of our work at home as well. No one would
disagree that daily chores are often monotonous, but we are
called to face them with a cheerful spirit. God will give us the
ability to do so when we ask Him.

Father, help me today to represent You well through my work.
I want to reflect Your love in all I do. Amen.

Godly Living in a Godless World

For the grace of God that bringeth salvation hath appeared to all men, teaching us that, denying ungodliness and worldly lusts, we should live soberly, righteously, and godly, in this present world.

TITUS 2:11–12 KJV

One of the most difficult tasks mothers have in the twenty-first century is teaching children godliness. We cannot go to a mall without being bombarded by ungodliness and worldly lusts. Innocence vanishes at the first lingerie store. The ubiquitous television and vile cable channels are a constant threat, as is the Internet with its "perversion on demand."

What's a woman to do?

Some have tried separation through home education. Others have cut the cable and filtered the Internet. Some avoid malls.

This is not enough. Keeping children unstained from the world alone will not foster godliness. Godliness is developed in children by careful, consistent training. Children must learn to obey parents, first time, every time, so that their hearts are ready to obey Christ.

Such training takes time and commitment. But it is our best investment against the ungodliness of the world.

Father, I put too much emphasis on the externals. I think that keeping the world out will develop godliness within. Help me give my children a pattern of obedience to follow. Amen.

A Mom, a Minivan,
and a Mercedes-Benz

*Has God forgotten to be gracious,
or has He in anger withdrawn His compassion?*

PSALM 77:9 NASB

A sporty Mercedes-Benz recklessly cut off Connie's mini-van as she was driving her son to basketball practice. At the school she noticed that Mr. Mercedes himself had parked and was walking toward the buildings.

Connie lowered her car window and politely asked, "Sir? Did you even realize that you cut me off?" The man stopped, narrowed his eyes, and swore at her.

Connie was stunned. How *dare* he treat a woman like that!

Sitting in the parking lot in shock, Connie prayed about the situation and it became clearer. It was as if the Lord was saying, "Stop personalizing this. Look beyond the behavior. Look at what it tells you about him."

Connie felt a wave of pity for the man. Anyone who would act that way, especially toward a mom in a minivan, must be a pretty miserable guy.

On his windshield Connie left a note, inviting him to church. *Who knows?* she thought. *Maybe he'll try it.*

*Lord, help me to turn to You even faster when I am upset or angry.
Thank You for intervening in my life and giving me the
perspective that I need.*

God could not be everywhere, and therefore
He made mothers.

RUDYARD KIPLING

God's Foolishness
Is Man's Wisdom

For the foolishness of God is wiser than man's wisdom,
and the weakness of God is stronger than man's strength.

1 CORINTHIANS 1:25 NIV

Cindy faced a troubling decision about her child. Which was the right path?

Finally, after time in prayer, she felt the Holy Spirit's prompting to move forward. The choice she felt led to make didn't entirely make sense—but she decided to follow the prompting anyway. Only afterward did she realize God had mysteriously guided her in the right decision.

God's directions don't always make sense. Did it "make sense" to have Jesus Christ die for our sins? How could a man, hanging on a cross outside Jerusalem, take away our sins? It's foolishness. Impossible!

But with God all things are possible. He asks us to simply take Him at His Word—and we have plenty of evidence, both biblical and physical, that shows us we can believe Him.

Believing God can seem like foolishness—at least in the world's eyes—but we know the deep peace that comes with that decision.

Lord, teach me to pray and to listen for Your guidance. I thank You that You go before me in every choice, even the confusing ones!

Love Is Patient

Love. . .is patient and kind.

1 CORINTHIANS 13:4 AMP

Why does the apostle Paul start his list of biblical characteristics of love with *patience*?

For most of us moms, that's the hardest quality of all.
What mother doesn't get exasperated when her kids dawdle,
drag their feet, and make her late? Who hasn't struggled
with their children's lack of initiative with schoolwork or
become irritated after the third time they tuck their children
into bed for the night?

But Paul says that love and patience are related. The
root word used in this biblical text refers to patience with
people, rather than patience with circumstances.

What happens when we are impatient with others? The
Bible tells us that impatience is ultimately caused by pride
(Ecclesiastes 7:8). And pride is the opposite of godly love.

God is patient with us and expects us, in turn, to be
patient with others. We don't give up on a child who frus-
trates or disappoints us. We hope for the best, we're quick to
forgive, and we work to keep our tongue reined in.

This is how true love behaves, Paul says. This love
reflects the very Author of love.

*Lord, remind me to turn ordinary annoyances into
opportunities in which I may honor and exalt You.*

A Pinch of Salt

Let your speech be alway with grace, seasoned with salt,
that ye may know how ye ought to answer every man.

COLOSSIANS 4:6 KJV

Recipes are detailed and specific, down to the tiniest dash of seasoning. It hardly seems possible that such a small amount of anything could affect the end result. But it does.

God has given us a recipe for Christian living. We are to be rich in grace, always ready to show love and mercy to others. But we are also to be "seasoned with salt." Without that seasoning, our silence around sin and bad behavior would be a subtle approval of things that grieve the heart of God.

For parents, that means we must sometimes lay aside our desire to be our child's "friend." We'll occasionally need to season our speech with enough salt to convey the truth of God's expectations.

But always remember: Grace is a vital part of making the saltiness palatable. Together grace and salt create a perfect dish that reveals the heart of God.

Lord, let my words and my life as a whole be pleasing
and effective in the lives of my children and others around me.

Clanging Cymbals

The quiet words of the wise are more effective
than the ranting of a king of fools.

ECCLESIASTES 9:17 MSG

One afternoon in a crowded department store, a five-year-old boy had a temper tantrum. A loud one! The boy's mom set aside her to-do list and focused on her out-of-control child. She crouched down to quietly speak with him in a soothing voice, and she calmed him down quite effectively.

That mom exhibited a wonderful model of good parenting for the wide-eyed bystanders. So often we witness the opposite kind of parenting. Rude put-downs, sharp words, threats of punishment. Parents can sound like clanging cymbals in the ears of their kids. Too often, especially when we're tired or stressed, *we* are guilty of that kind of parenting!

God has a better way for us to parent, even in the midst of temper tantrums in public places. That wise mom in the store gave a snapshot of how God gently parents us! He is infinitely patient, speaks with a loving voice, and gives His complete attention despite our embarrassing meltdowns.

Lord of Lords, when I need to discipline my kids, help me to check
my tone of voice and my expression. Bring to mind
Your definition of true love: It is patient, kind, and never rude.

The Least of These

The king will answer, "Whenever you did it for any of my people, no matter how unimportant they seemed, you did it for me."

MATTHEW 25:40 CEV

Some people act as if children are something to be tolerated, not cultivated. They are signed up for this, dropped off for that, and somehow, in the course of all of the activity, they are supposed to learn and grow into adults with a sense of thoughtful purpose. Do we think they'll teach themselves?

Jesus understood the potential of each child. He knew that their little hearts and minds were hungry for knowledge and truth. He knew that their training was an investment in the future of the Kingdom of God.

We may never know the full scope of our impact on our own kids, but we are definitely part of God's plan for the development of their young lives. As a mother you have the potential to bless a child's life forever.

And according to the Lord Himself, whatever you do for a child, you do for Him.

Jesus, use me to shape the lives of my children for Your glory. Help me to see these kids as a gift from You—never as a hindrance to my adult pursuits. Please grant me Your wisdom and love.

Every mother is like Moses.
She does not enter the Promised Land.
She prepares a world she will not see.

POPE PAUL VI

Faith

Faith Eyes

*Now faith is being sure of what we hope
for and certain of what we do not see.*

HEBREWS 11:1 NIV

Think for a moment of things we can't see but we know are there.

There's the wind, for one. Its effects are obvious on fields of golden grain and autumn forests. And there's gravity, which pulls our kids' cups—full of red Kool-Aid, usually—right to the floor.

It's the same with faith: God *says* He is faithful, and so His faithfulness exists. He gives us the signs of His unseen presence, and its effects surround us.

We read how, at Moses' command, the Red Sea parted. The Israelites could have been killed, but God made a safe way of escape for them.

What signs surround you, showing you God is real? Perhaps someone blessed you with money to pay a bill. Maybe your "guardian angel" caught your attention and helped you avoid a serious accident. Or perhaps your child prayed to accept the Lord.

Look around with your "faith eyes" and see the signs surrounding you.

God, I struggle to have faith. Show me where You have been faithful so my faith can be strengthened. I need a special sign that You have not forgotten me. Thank You, Father.

More Faith

We live by faith, not by sight.
2 CORINTHIANS 5:7 NIV

Faith is a word often carelessly used. People—rich and poor, single and married, content and miserable—randomly toss the mysterious term around. But what is faith, really? It's believing in something without first having to prove it.

Imagine this scene: At a family barbeque, you watch in mock horror as Aunt Sally plops herself onto an unsteady lawn chair—only to have it fold in on itself, spewing the red-faced woman onto the lawn. Amazingly, after she peels herself off the ground and finds some composure, she snaps open *another* chair and sits right down, trusting this one will support her. "We live by faith, not by sight."

Faith is what we have in Christ. Our daily circumstances may point to failure and frustration, but faith says God has all things under control—and He never fails. Even when it seems like we are drowning, He will lift us up, keep us strong, and put a song in our heart.

Lord, I need more faith. I know You will never leave me or forget about my troubles. Life seems overwhelming at times, so I ask You to increase my faith in You.

A Block of Marble

*I praise you because I am fearfully and wonderfully made;
your works are wonderful, I know that full well.*

PSALM 139:14 NIV

In 1501 Michelangelo looked at a block of marble and saw "David." Three years later Michelangelo chiseled out his masterpiece. He worked under an artistic discipline called *disegno*: the belief that the art was already inside the block of marble.

That's a picture of how God sees us! With His divine genius, God made us purposefully with loving intention. "For you created my inmost being; you knit me together in my mother's womb," wrote King David in Psalm 139:13 (NIV).

We look at ourselves and see the uncut sections, the rough edges, the areas that need sanding and polishing. Will we ever be considered a work of art? We seem like such a mess. But God looks at us and sees the sculpted piece, His completed masterpiece!

Do we see our children in the same way that God sees us? Or the way Michelangelo looked at a block of marble and saw "David?" Our children are miracles, filled with possibilities! God is accomplishing a soon-to-be revealed masterpiece through them.

Dear Lord, how awesome is Your artistry! Open my eyes to Your creative ways. Give me Your vision to see my children's potential.

Pass It On

*You must be very careful not to forget the things you
have seen God do for you. Keep reminding yourselves,
and tell your children and grandchildren as well.*

DEUTERONOMY 4:9 CEV

Why don't we throw this old thing away?" nine-year-old
Crystal asked, gingerly fingering the worn wood of the
rustic three-legged stool. "It must be fifty years old."

"Actually, it's almost eighty years old," Dina told her
daughter. "And I wouldn't dream of throwing it away. In
fact, I've taken special care of it my entire life, as my mother
did, and her father before her."

"Why would you want to keep an old stool?"

"It's more than just an old stool. It's a symbol of God's
grace to our family. That was the first piece of furniture your
great-grandfather owned when he arrived in our country
after fleeing the Nazi occupation of Poland. That stool represents the answered prayers and provision of God for our
family through the years, even down to you, Crystal. It helps
us remember to thank God for the blessings He's given us."

"Oh, I see. It's kind of like wearing a cross pendant to
remember Jesus dying for us." Crystal tenderly ran her hand
over the rough wood with new respect. "I'll keep it for my
children, too."

God created families, and it was His plan that we share
His workings in our lives with generations yet to come.

*Rock of Ages, help us always to remember Your loving kindnesses
and pass the word on to those who share our genes, blood, and
even our knobby knees. Amen.*

So, Talk!

No one is able to come to Me unless the Father Who sent Me attracts and draws him and gives him the desire to come to Me.

JOHN 6:44 AMP

In some of the psalms, the writers seem to shake their fists at God, shouting, "Where are You, Lord? Why are You so slow? Are You sleeping? Wake up and help me!"

Fortunately for us human beings, God isn't easily offended. He is deeply committed to holding up His end of our relationship, and He doesn't want us to hide anything from Him. He already knows every thought we have, anyway. Why not talk to Him about those thoughts?

Our Father always wants to talk. In fact, the very impulse to pray originates in God. In his book *The Pursuit of God*, author A. W. Tozer wrote, "We pursue God because, and only because, He has first put an urge within us that spurs us to the pursuit."

So, talk!

Lord God, it boggles my mind that You want to hear from me! Your Word says that I can call out Your name with confidence. That You will answer me! Today, Lord, I give You praise—and my heart's deepest longings.

As a mother, my job is to take care of what is possible and trust God with the impossible.

RUTH BELL GRAHAM

Futile Faith?

We clean the windows and wash the car, and a day later it rains. We sweep the kitchen floor, and hours later the crunch of cookie crumbs resounds under our feet. Some tasks seem so futile.

So it is with our spiritual life. We pray unceasingly, and no answers seem to come; or we work tirelessly, and problems entrench us. In frustration we wonder, *Why did this happen? What purpose is there to all of this?* It all seems so pointless.

But even when our prayers remain unanswered, we continue to pray. Even when God is silent, we continue to believe. And though we grope for answers, we continue to trust.

When our chaotic lives turn upside down and we labor to find rhyme and reason, God asks us to hold fast to our faith. For no labor of love is pointless; no prayer is futile.

Dear Lord, please forgive me for allowing my problems to undermine my faith. I trust in You, knowing that my faith in You is never futile. Amen.

Who Am I?

Then he asked them, "But who do you say I am?"
Peter replied, "You are the Messiah."

MARK 8:29 NLT

Mom, Mama, Mother—whatever our children call us, it's
the most precious sound on earth. We remember the first
time our babies called us "Mama" and noted the occasion
in their baby books. As time passes, they begin to recognize
our other roles: Christian. . .employee. . .daughter. . .church
member. . .friend.

In a similar way we see God first as a Father—and
when we lisp "Daddy" to Him, it's as precious to His ears
as "Mama" is to ours. But while God is a loving, heavenly
Father, He is also much more.

When we pray, let's stop to consider Jesus' question,
"Who do you say that I am?"

Perhaps, with Peter, we'll affirm, "You are the promised Messiah, my Savior." When we can't imagine how our
topsy-turvy circumstances will work out, we'll call Him
"Alpha and Omega," the One who began everything and
will still be there throughout eternity.

Who is God to us today? We can't go wrong meditating
on His many names.

Lord God, teach me to recognize that everything I want or need
I find in You. Thank You for revealing Yourself to me.

Why Pray?

"Why were you searching for Me?" He asked them.
"Didn't you know that I had to be in my Father's house?"

LUKE 2:49 HCSB

Most of us have heard the story. Mary and Joseph unknowingly leave the twelve-year-old Jesus behind in Jerusalem. They spend a frantic three days looking for him. Finally found in the temple, Jesus responds with an interesting question: "Why were you searching for Me?"

What makes us seek God out? Perhaps, like Mary and Joseph, we've missed our connection with the Lord for a few days. God may seem far away, though *He* hasn't moved. We are the ones who seem to have lost our way.

Maybe we're rushing to God because we're worried. Or perhaps we're doubting God's goodness. We might repeat the anxious question of Mary and Joseph in our prayers: "Why have You treated us like this?" (Luke 2:48 HCSB). When we hurl anger at God, He simply absorbs it, reprimands or encourages us as needed, and renews our strength for another day.

So why do we pray? There are as many reasons as there are minutes in the day.

Heavenly Father, I know that when I seek You, I will find You.
I praise You and pray that I will learn to come to
You with every detail of my life.

Christmas List

Many children eagerly wait for holiday toy catalogs to arrive. They may sit with copies spread across their laps, carefully marking the items they wish to receive for Christmas.

Parents generally take those lists and catalog markings very seriously. They *want* to give their children the things their little hearts most desire, especially at Christmastime when a little indulgence is welcomed. They don't scowl at their children, telling them to stop being greedy. Instead they delight in the expectation and joy they see on their children's faces.

When we pray, it's as though *we* are making a Christmas list. But it's not just one time a year that our Father is prepared to fulfill our needs and wants. He enjoys every opportunity to pour out His richest blessings on us, His children.

Our heavenly Father wants us to approach Him with expectation, knowing that every good and perfect gift comes from Him.

Heavenly Father, I thank You for Your rich blessings
and treasured gifts. Thank You for hearing my
prayers and eagerly providing for me.

Warm Fuzzies

You are near, O Lord [nearer to me than my foes], and all Your commandments are truth. . . . The sum of Your word is truth.

PSALM 119:151, 160 AMP

Have you ever read a scripture and thought, *That's nice. . .but is it real?*

At times we're all tempted to think God might try to placate His children with tales of comfort or miracles that don't ring true with our day-to-day experience. But that's not the case at all. Whether we need money for groceries or comfort for a broken heart, child care or a car that runs, vindication or a vacation. . .God provides real substance—not just warm fuzzies.

God will never tell us, "It'll be okay," when it won't. Though He may not remove our difficulties, He has promised to be with us in the midst of them and walk us through to the other side.

As the psalms tell us, God's Word is the sum of Truth. Trusting that Word is much more than a positive thinking exercise. . . . It is our faith in action.

Father God, what a comfort it is to know that You aren't simply trying to give me a warm, fuzzy feeling. You care for me and are faithful to walk me through whatever I face.

A mother's love perceives no impossibilities.

CORNELIA PADDOCK

The Forever Word

"The grass withers and the flowers fall,
but the word of our God stands forever."

ISAIAH 40:8 NIV

There is nothing more powerful, more honest, more lasting, or more truthful than God's Word. Grass withers in the summer heat; flowers die and fall to the ground at their season's end. Even our precious children grow up, eventually leaving the nest to venture into the world without us.

The one thing that never changes—that's consistently the same yesterday, today, and for all eternity—is the Word of our God. Wherever we keep God's Word—on fragile onionskinned paper or on the Internet—we find life. We find the God-inspired guidance, understanding, and wisdom we need to raise our children well.

When we study God's Word wholeheartedly, He will illuminate it, giving us an understanding that brings perfect peace. While everything around us changes, we can rest in the one thing that stands forever—the true, unchanging Word of God.

Lord Jesus, I thank You for Your Word. I pray that
You would teach me more and more how to obtain
its nourishment and wisdom for my spirit. I ask
You to bless me with greater understanding.

Always?

*Always be joyful. Never stop praying. Be thankful in all
circumstances, for this is God's will for you
who belong to Christ Jesus.*

1 THESSALONIANS 5:16–18 NLT

Why is it so hard to pray?

Maybe our own mediocre experience with prayer hurts us. Sometimes we bore ourselves! We get easily distracted. It can be difficult to even get started. Words fail us.

Keeping a prayer notebook and using it during quiet time—with prayers written out and dated—is one way of enriching our prayer lives.

What are the advantages of a prayer journal? It can help us realize that God has answered more prayers than we think. It can remind us to lift up people in ongoing circumstances, because we're prone to forget. It can broaden our objectivity, especially important for moms as we lift up our concerns over our kids and allow His light to shine on our problems. And it can train us in the habit of prayer as a first and immediate response to our family joys and crises alike.

*Lord, how good it is to know that when mothers pray,
we can be confident our prayers are received
and attended to by a loving Father.*

Untidy Prayers

"When you pray, do not say the same thing over and over again making long prayers like the people who do not know God. They think they are heard because their prayers are long. Do not be like them. Your Father knows what you need before you ask Him."

MATTHEW 6:7–8 NLV

When our child falls down, scrapes a knee, and calls out our name, what do we do? We hear that desperate need in his voice. We hear and respond immediately.

God is no different.

The Lord loves prayers that burst out of a hurting heart. Those prayers are authentic, sincere, earnest. Consider how many of David's psalms begin with a cry from the depths of his very human soul.

The Lord listens to those in need (Psalm 69:33). We can pray simple, untidy, not fancy, from-the-gut prayers and know God will not be shocked.

God isn't like the grocery cashier who keeps his eyes lowered, mumbling, "How are you today?" God *really* wants to know. What's on your mind? Tell God! He already knows our real thoughts and feelings, but He still longs to hear from us.

Father in heaven, You gave us ears, both physical and spiritual. I thank You for the gift of two-way conversations with You.

Faith Fitness

Ye, beloved, building up yourselves on your most holy faith,
praying in the Holy Ghost, keep yourselves in the love of God,
looking for the mercy of our Lord Jesus Christ unto eternal life.

JUDE 20–21 KJV

Physical fitness takes center stage in our country. Stores teem with books full of advice to help us look better, feel stronger, and live longer. Everyone wears workout suits and jogging shoes. Thousands of dollars are spent on exercise equipment and gym memberships.

So we can conclude all Americans are physically fit, right?

Unfortunately our interest does not necessarily transfer to our actions. Judging from the number of sports channels, we love to watch other people exercise, but sweating it out ourselves? That's a whole other ball game.

In the same way, we Christians often fall short in building ourselves up spiritually. We buy millions of Bibles and tons of literature, attend conferences and seminars—but we don't practice daily spiritual disciplines that make us strong. Jude, the half-brother of Jesus, urges us to devote time and energy to fervent prayer in the Spirit. Exercising our faith like this daily will keep us fit for God's heavenly purpose.

Lord, help me stay on top of my spiritual, as well as physical,
conditioning. Thanks for Your concern for me.

Share the News

I pray that you may be active in sharing your faith, so that you will have a full understanding of every good thing we have in Christ.

PHILEMON 1:6 NIV

Joy was awaiting takeoff. She was headed toward home—and her children—after a weeklong business trip. This was a chance for a little shut-eye before seeing her family once again.

Joy was about to doze off when a talkative woman sat down in the next seat. It didn't take long for Joy to realize her traveling partner needed to hear the good news about Jesus Christ. *Not today, God,* Joy thought—but she knew this was an opening she had to take.

Sharing our faith with others can be scary, but we could also help lead someone to Jesus. Either way we must share the good news.

When we get excited about other important things in our lives—our children's accomplishments, a new job—we share them with others. How much more important it is—and how much more joy we'll get—sharing Christ's love with others.

Share that news! The reward is so much greater than the risk.

Father, You have given me so many blessings—please help me to share Your love and goodness with others.